Beatrice Cenci

ALBERTO MORAVIA

Beatrice Cenci

Translated from the Italian
by Angus Davidson

The Noonday Press,
a division of Farrar, Straus & Giroux
New York

DRAMATIS PERSONAE

Francesco Cenci

Olimpio Calvetti
Governor of the Castle of La Petrella

Marzio Catalano
A teacher of the guitar

Carlo Tirone
Chief Justice of the Province of the Abruzzi

Beatrice
Daughter of Francesco

Lucrezia
Francesco's second wife

The action takes place in the main room of the castle
of La Petrella, in the Abruzzi, in the year 1598

ACT ONE

SCENE 1

BEATRICE, LUCREZIA AND MARZIO

(The main room in the Castle of La Petrella. An enormous hall with a ceiling of roughly whitewashed beams. The walls are dirty, blackened by smoke from the fire and by years of neglect. On the walls are trophies of the chase, one or two cupboards and a few pictures. A great stone fireplace, with two or three large chairs round it. A few other pieces of massive, rustic furniture. There are three great windows at the back, with deep embrasures which convey the feeling of the walls' great thickness.

At the moment when the curtain rises, Lucrezia and Beatrice are sitting at a large table in the middle of the room, both of them occupied with needlework. The windows are shut, and through the panes snow can be seen falling. In the fireplace a fire of huge logs is blazing. Beatrice and Lucrezia are dressed in rags. In front of the fire sits Marzio, a guitar across his knees. Marzio's clothes, too, are ragged.)

LUCREZIA: All night long it was snowing. A month ago there was rain. And a few months ago there was sunshine. It seems to me I have been up here for centuries.

9

BEATRICE: You never cease complaining—to us who can do nothing. But when my father is here you are silent. (*To Marzio*): Are you quite sure you handed the letter to my brother?

LUCREZIA: You've already asked him and he has already answered you.

BEATRICE: Please allow me to ask him that question as often as I like. It costs him nothing to answer, and his answer gives me pleasure.

MARZIO: I went straight to the palace, as soon as I reached Rome. I asked for your brother and handed him the letter, requesting him not to show it to Lord Francesco, as you bade me. He opened it in my presence, read it, and then said: "I wish to show this letter to my uncle. In the meantime tell my sister to set her mind at rest; and tell her also that something will be done for her as soon as possible."

BEATRICE: He really said that?

MARZIO: Those were his words.

BEATRICE: And when was it you handed him the letter?

MARZIO: It was on the 3rd of December—Wednesday.

BEATRICE: And today is the 10th. By this time there should have been some sign of Giacomo and my uncle. However, it's winter, and the weather is bad and the roads muddy; it's quite possible they've been delayed. What do you think? (*To Lucrezia*).

LUCREZIA: Ah, my child, it is difficult for those who are happy to understand those who are not.

BEATRICE: What do you mean by that?

LUCREZIA: Your letter told him the truth—that the life we lead up here is worse than death. But what is that to your brother and your uncle? They live in Rome, in comfortable houses, with their wives, free to do whatever they like. No doubt they said, at the moment: yes, something must be done for those poor women. And then no doubt they did nothing—as usual.

BEATRICE: Do you believe that?

LUCREZIA: I do not believe it; but I fear it.

BEATRICE (*rising in great agitation, to Marzio*): But you heard my brother say: "Something shall be done for her"? You heard him say that?

MARZIO: Ah, you grieve me by doubting me! Certainly he said that.

BEATRICE: Truly I feel I shall commit some act of folly. These days of waiting have worn me out: always looking out of the window to see if they're coming, always hoping in vain! I shall commit some act of folly—yes, I shall throw myself down from the battlements, and then, for me, it will all be over, and this is what my father wanted and he will be pleased, and for you, too, it will be better, because it is on my account that he keeps you up here, because he does not want me to marry.

LUCREZIA: Calm yourself, I beg you. And take no notice of me; I am discouraged and do not know what I am saying. Of course they will come. In fact, I have a presentiment that all things will improve in a short time from now. I have my reasons for believing this.

BEATRICE: What reasons?

LUCREZIA: It was told me by a gipsy-woman who came up to the castle this morning. She looked at my hand and then she consulted the cards, and she said to me: "Changes, great changes in the house."

BEATRICE: Oh, so you believe in gipsies.

MARZIO: Many secrets are known to the gipsies, Lady Beatrice.

BEATRICE: You think so?

MARZIO: Certainly I do. They foretold that my wife would have a boy child on such-and-such a day of such-and-such a month. And it all came true to the last detail.

BEATRICE: Oh Marzio, dear Marzio, would to God it may be so! So earnestly have I prayed to God to grant my request.

MARZIO (*rising and going to the window*): God will grant your request. (*After a moment, as he looks out, with a cry*): Lady Beatrice, God *is* granting your request.

BEATRICE: What do you say?

MARZIO: Come and look yourself. Do you see, down there on the road, close to that group of trees —do you see those two black spots moving? It's two men on horseback and they're coming up here. And who can it be but your brother and your uncle?

(*Beatrice and Lucrezia go over to the window and look out.*)

LUCREZIA: Yes, I see them too. It's two men on horseback. And one of them is Giacomo, I'm sure; I recognize him.

BEATRICE: All I see is two black spots.

LUCREZIA: Now they're starting to circle round the castle. There, they've disappeared! Soon they'll be here.

BEATRICE: I can't believe it. Marzio, do go quickly on to the terrace; go and see if it's really those two.

MARZIO: If it is, I'll go and meet them and bring them back along the road playing and singing and dancing in the snow. (*He takes up his guitar and goes out.*)

SCENE 2

BEATRICE: Do you think it is Giacomo and my uncle?

LUCREZIA: I don't think so, I am sure of it: I recognized them.

BEATRICE: Yes, surely it must be, it cannot be anyone else. Not village people; they would be on foot. Not strangers, for no one comes this way in the winter. Not my father either, because he wrote that he would not come before Easter and he is not given to changing his mind. So it cannot be anyone else. And if it is Giacomo and my uncle, they can only have come all this way in order to fetch us and take us back to Rome. We shall go to Rome, I shall go to Rome! And once I am back in Rome, I refuse to submit any longer to my father's madness. During these two years that I've spent up here in the castle, it's true that I've suffered, but I've also gained in strength, and now I know quite well what I want. Once I am back in Rome, I shall put myself under the protection of my uncle, who loves me. And I shall persuade him to find me a husband as soon as possible. I want a husband who loves me and whom I can love, a husband who can promise me the kind of life I have a right to, according to my position. I want a palace, a coach, horses, servants; fine frescoed rooms to live in, in the winter, with the rest of the family, and a beautiful garden to walk in in the summer. And I want to give balls and parties and to entertain according to my rank; I want my parties to be among the finest in Rome. And I want all Rome to come and visit me and I want people to talk of me as one of the greatest ladies of the city. I want painters to make portraits of me and musicians to enliven me with their airs, and I want many learned men to come to my house and instruct me in the sublime problems of their philosophy, and to discuss them amongst themselves and with me. I want all life to be a feast, a dance, a piece of music, a light breeze to carry away the days, one after the other, without sorrow or pain. Oh, I want to be truly a great lady! And also I want to travel with my husband and to go to Venice and then to Paris and be presented at Court there. And when I come in front of the King of France, I'll curtsey like this (*she curtseys*) and like that, and as I do so Their Majesties will say to each other in a whisper: "How beautiful she is, this Roman lady!" Come, Lucrezia, come and embrace me—I'm happy! (*Beatrice forces Lucrezia to get up and go dancing round the room with her.*)

LUCREZIA: Let me go, you're crazy. You have far too much imagination. As for me, all I want is to go back to Rome and live quietly there in my own house. All that pomp and grandeur is not for me.

BEATRICE: Without grandeur, life has no savour, Lucrezia. And I—I am born for everything that is grand and noble and beautiful and pure and joyful.

SCENE 3

BEATRICE, LUCREZIA AND MARZIO

MARZIO (*enters in great haste*): We are betrayed! Betrayed!

LUCREZIA: What is it?

MARZIO: I went out on to the terrace and looked. And I recognized them. It is *not* Lord Giacomo and his uncle.

LUCREZIA: Who is it, then?

MARZIO: Lord Francesco and Olimpio. They will be here in a moment. (*There follows a long silence. The two women seem turned to stone.*)

MARZIO: Yet it may possibly have happened that Lord Francesco somehow got possession of the letter and, after reading it, decided at last to come up here and repair the wrong he has done and take you back to Rome. Who knows?

BEATRICE (*advancing suddenly to the fireplace and seizing the poker*): Be silent! And go—or I'll kill you!

MARZIO: Have mercy, Lady Beatrice!

LUCREZIA: Calm yourself! Possibly Marzio may be right. After all, Francesco is your father and . . .

BEATRICE: Oh, let me alone! (*She throws down the poker and leaves the room.*)

MARZIO: It is no fault of mine. I handed over the letter to Lord Giacomo, he read it and said he would do something. How the letter can have come into the hands of Lord Francesco, really I do not know.

LUCREZIA: I am going to see where Beatrice has gone. I would not want her through disappointment really to do something foolish. (*Exit.*)

SCENE 4

Olimpio and Marzio

(*Olimpio enters, shaking the snow from his hat. He is dressed for travelling.*)

OLIMPIO: Marzio, good day! No news?

MARZIO: The only news is your arrival.

OLIMPIO: News for everyone else—but not for you, Marzio. And how is our lovely child?

MARZIO: To her own way of thinking, she is ill; to yours, she is well.

OLIMPIO: Is she very desperate?

MARZIO: Exceedingly desperate she was, so much so that she made me carry that letter. And in the letter she said, in fact, that she was so desperate that she felt capable of committing some act of folly. But she did not say what, and I do not think she was alluding to the act of folly you would like her to commit.

OLIMPIO: In certain states of mind, one act of folly is as good as another. And people always end by committing the one that's handiest and easiest and most convenient.

19

Marzio: She was hoping that her brother and uncle would come and fetch her and take her back to Rome. A short time ago she looked out of the window and thought she recognized them. So she was filled with joy and excitement. Then she learned that it was you and Lord Francesco, and from the heights of joy she plunged into an abyss of despair. Indeed I believe that at this moment she is more desperate than she was when you left her, if that is possible.

Olimpio: Excellent, that is what is wanted: an alternation between hope and despair which will break her heart in the end, and make her ready to accept anything.

Marzio: You are counting a little too much upon despair as your natural ally. Be careful that the alternation you speak of does not go beyond the mark.

Olimpio: Why? It is true that she will give herself to me from sheer despair. But once she has given herself to me, her despair will come to an end, and she will have something to think about and something to live for.

Marzio: A love that is born of despair cannot, as far as I can see, ever be a real love. Besides, I tell you truly, Olimpio, when I saw her so desperate, when I reflected that, in order to give you pleasure, I had deceived her and had handed the letter to her father instead of her brother, I was seized with remorse. It is an evil deed that we have done. And no good can come from an evil deed.

OLIMPIO: Let us not talk of good or evil deeds. Let us look rather at our motives: and you had a good motive for doing what you did, Marzio. The money I gave you will be useful to your family.

MARZIO: That is true, but . . .

OLIMPIO: There's no "but" about it; it's a good motive. And for my part, Marzio, I also had a good motive for doing what I did—passion. This too, Marzio, is a good motive, an excellent motive.

MARZIO: Perhaps it may be. But all the same, when I think of what is bound to happen here in a short time, because of you and me; when I think of what her father will say and do to her—I cannot help feeling remorse. And besides, as I have already told you, I do not want her despair to go too far, beyond the limit of what is useful to you. What would you do with a woman who preferred death to a life without hope? Would you speak to her, then, of your passion?

OLIMPIO: Things have now reached a point when I want her at any cost, dead or alive. But I have thought of that too. And I intend—yes, I intend that her father shall go on keeping her up here, giving her no hope of escape, but not that he shall ill-treat her to the point of making her wish for death. She must be just desperate enough to fall into my arms, but not more. I shall contrive somehow to check her father, Marzio.

MARZIO: I do not know what you can do. Poisons, even, can be tempered, but not the fury of a man like that. There will always be more of that fury in him than you desire for your own purposes.

OLIMPIO: I have already considered that. As we came up here, I sought to mollify the cold rigidity of his fury. Several times I dropped a remark such as: "Lord Francesco, you should be satisfied with keeping her at the Castle for a few months longer or at most another year or two—not more." Or: "Her disobedience has certainly earned her a long stay at the Castle, but not that you should punish her in any other way." Or again: "If I were in your place, Lord Francesco, I shouldn't say anything to her; I should simply announce, in a casual way: 'It's understood, of course, that you are to stay at the Castle for another year'."

MARZIO: And he—what answer did he make?

OLIMPIO: No answer at all. He rode like a demon, head down and teeth clenched, and never opened his mouth.

MARZIO: You see? What did I tell you?

OLIMPIO: Yes, but it's impossible to tell what effect my words had upon him: he certainly heard them.

Moreover, I'm now going to contrive to speak to him before he sees Beatrice, and again I shall try to calm his anger. Above all, Marzio, he pays attention to me and is fond of me and always asks my advice. I am sure he will listen to me again this time.

MARZIO: He does not listen to his own conscience; why in the world should he listen to you?

OLIMPIO: Ha, seldom do men listen to their own consciences. But if consciences put on clothes and carried swords and rode in coaches, they would listen to them more.

MARZIO: That may be so. But I do not wish to see him, whatever may be the effect of your advice upon him. That man makes me afraid. (*Exit.*)

SCENE 5

Francesco and Olimpio

(Enter Francesco. He also is in travelling dress. He goes straight to the fireplace and stretches out his hands to the flames.)

Francesco: So here we are. You see, Olimpio: you said we should not do it in two days—instead of which, we left on the 8th and today is the 10th and it's still morning.

Olimpio: Lord Francesco, we did it because you rode like a demon and exhausted the horses. What I said was that, at a normal pace, it would take three days.

Francesco: Well, anyhow, I've won my bet and you owe me five *scudi*.

Olimpio: I'll give them to you as soon as I can. I have them at home.

Francesco: Never mind. Give them to me when you can. But don't imagine I am letting you off your debt: you owe me five *scudi*.

Olimpio: I have always paid my debts.

FRANCESCO: Well and good, then. (*Francesco leaves the fireplace, goes over to the window and looks out.*) I could not have endured to stay in Rome any longer. I was dying of boredom there, and yawning myself into a state of exhaustion; and in the mornings, when I woke up and looked out of the window of my room, I longed for the earth to have swallowed up the house opposite during the night, so that I might be spared the sight of its cracks and patches of damp, of its windows and cornices. But now, no sooner have I arrived here than the mere sight of the snow falling on the roofs of these wretched shepherds' hovels brings back my boredom again, worse than in Rome. Are you never bored, Olimpio?

OLIMPIO: There's always plenty to do up here, my Lord. Sometimes it happens that I get bored, too, but rarely. I was more often bored as a young man, when I was a soldier.

FRANCESCO: It is true that what I call boredom is really something that only the devil can explain. You see, my dear Olimpio, this boredom that afflicts me is a thing that you cannot understand because you have a more youthful and a richer blood in your veins than I have, and that house in Rome that causes me so much pain when I look at it from the window would no doubt appear to you beautiful and strong and without any cracks in it. What I do is to deceive myself into thinking that boredom lies in external things, whereas really it is in my own dulled senses that can only be roused by the strongest sensations. Ah, Olimpio, life should be all made up of intense, of painful moments; then perhaps this boredom would disappear. But already you cannot understand me. So little bored are you that you can still find the strength to pretend, and to present me with a dutiful and devoted picture of yourself. But a man who is bored—the first thing he does is to send politeness to the devil.

OLIMPIO: My Lord Francesco, between you and me there is a difference.

FRANCESCO: And that is——?

OLIMPIO: That I am dependent upon you, and a dependant neither can nor ought ever to be bored.

FRANCESCO: Perhaps you are right. I am dependent upon nobody, and precisely for that reason I am dependent upon boredom, or rather, upon the need to give a jolt to my senses which seem, every moment, to be failing and thus breaking my contact with external things. You see, Olimpio, this boredom lies in my incapacity to feel myself alive in quiet, normal, ordinary conditions. And in order to feel myself alive, then . . .

OLIMPIO: Then?

FRANCESCO: What are all those people doing—coming out of the village at this moment and walking in single file over the snow?

OLIMPIO: Ha, those people aren't bored, they haven't the time. They are going to the wood to get logs for cooking and heating. If they don't go, they die of hunger and cold.

FRANCESCO: Necessity: perhaps that's the secret of not being bored. And boredom would mean absence of necessity, availability, freedom of choice. No, no: I too have my own necessity—to jolt my senses in some way or other, to feel myself alive. And to live, to feel that he lives, is surely man's first necessity; isn't that so, Olimpio?

OLIMPIO: My Lord Franscesco, allow me to be frank with you.

FRANCESCO: Frank? You—frank? You want to change your name?

OLIMPIO: Forgive me—I don't understand you.

FRANCESCO: You want to change your name: to be Frank with me and Olimpio with other people?

OLIMPIO: You always like making jokes, my Lord.

FRANCESCO: It's you who likes making jokes, Olimpio. To be frank with me? That's really a joke!

OLIMPIO: And why?

FRANCESCO: You claim you would be telling me the truth about myself, or at least what you think is the truth. With others that might perhaps be a useful undertaking, but not with me.

OLIMPIO: Not with you?

FRANCESCO: No. And for the very good reason that I know all about myself, the whole truth.

OLIMPIO: We never know enough about ourselves, my Lord.

FRANCESCO: Don't trouble yourself about that. Do you want a proof? I will tell you now what it was you had in mind to tell me when you offered me your frankness. In return I ask only one thing from you: to tell me—in all frankness, of course—whether I have guessed right. If I have not guessed right, well— I'll let you off that debt of five *scudi*.

OLIMPIO: Agreed.

FRANCESCO: Well, let's see, then. To put it briefly, what you meant to say to me was this: you say you are bored, but that is not really the point; you are one of the cruellest and most corrupt men in Rome.

OLIMPIO: Ah no. I didn't mean to say that.

FRANCESCO: Don't trouble yourself about it, I tell you; that was what you meant to say, though in different words. But wait, I have not finished. What you meant to say to me was, in short, this: Lord

Francesco, you are known in Rome for your cruelty and your corruption. You beat your servants, your wife, your daughter, and anyone who has the misfortune to incur your anger. Furthermore, you force the women in your house to do your pleasure, and the men too, without distinction of age or condition, or of sex. Your vices are famous, and you have been thrown into prison several times for these vices and have been able to get out again only by paying very heavy fines, so that you are now ruined. Finally, you do not live as a nobleman should: your palace is a bare and gloomy cavern, full of broken furniture and filth and misery, and in this abode you associate with serving-girls of the lowest class, with grooms, pimps, harlots, usurers and cut-throats. You are lustful, violent, miserly, untruthful, unjust and treacherous; there is nothing noble, and nothing good, in your life. Everything in it is loathsome and perverse and false. Isn't that right, my dearest Olimpio? Isn't that what you wanted to say to me, Olimpio?

OLIMPIO: Forgive me, Lord Francesco; but really this was not the point.

FRANCESCO: Gently now, I'm coming to the point. Here, in fact, is the point. After drawing this picture of me, you had it in mind to say to me: and in spite of all this you're bored. Why then don't you try a change of system? It might happen that, if you were good and upright, honest, generous, mild and reasonable, and if you lived as a nobleman should, you might cease to be bored. Well, Olimpio, that was your idea—isn't that so, Olimpio?

OLIMPIO: Partly—yes. You are very clever, Lord Francesco, and . . .

FRANCESCO: Let's cut out the flattery.

OLIMPIO: Well then, seeing that you know yourself so well, why . . . ?

FRANCESCO: One moment. I did not say that I was bored when—to take an example—I am beating my wife. I said I was bored when I got up in the morning and went to the window and looked at the façade of the house opposite.

OLIMPIO: I no longer understand what you mean.

FRANCESCO: Indeed how could you understand? In spite of your military career and your killings and your heroics, you are a very moderate, a very sober, a very reasonable man, Olimpio. You may know how to use a dagger—but only for an injury received, for a calculated reason, for a motive, in fact.

OLIMPIO: We all act with some motive or other. Even you, Lord Francesco.

FRANCESCO: Are you quite sure of that? Anyhow, you have admitted that I read your thoughts to perfection. And now I will answer you just as if you had been really frank with me. In the first place: don't you know that once upon a time I was exactly like other noblemen of my rank?

OLIMPIO: I have never known you otherwise than as you now are.

FRANCESCO: Because you have known me only for a short time. But at twenty I was different, Olimpio. I was exactly the kind of nobleman you would like to turn me into now, when I'm fifty. I have already done everything you would like me to do. I have been polite and accomplished and charming, and like all noblemen of my age and rank I sang and danced and wrote poems, I frequented artists and men of learning and paid court to beautiful Roman ladies, one of whom I finally married and by her had the children I now have. And, like any self-respecting nobleman, I was also pious. Yes, Olimpio, I was pious, I performed good works, I distributed alms, I was the benefactor of convents. In the years of my early manhood I did all these things and many other things too, all of them praiseworthy. But the boredom, Olimpio, the boredom of all that!

OLIMPIO: And yet that is the way noblemen should live.

FRANCESCO: Yes, but I did not wish to be a dead nobleman so much as a live man. And then I discovered by chance that all the good and praiseworthy things I did were killing me, whereas their opposites restored me to life. I could even tell you how I discovered this; but confidences must have a limit. You must be satisfied with knowing this much: that I abandoned myself to what you call my vices, because I found that these vices gave me a jolt and drove out the boredom from my mind.

OLIMPIO: Lord Francesco, a man can be a worthy nobleman and yet, if he is restrained and discreet, take some pleasure with women and wine and gambling, and so on. One thing does not exclude the other.

FRANCESCO: Always reasonable, always sober, always moderate—our dear good Olimpio! And of course you are right: a man can be a worthy nobleman and at the same time quite the opposite—provided, always, he is restrained and discreet. Why not, indeed? But my case is different, Olimpio.

OLIMPIO: Again I must confess I don't understand you.

FRANCESCO: Better that you shouldn't, because I am not entrusting you with confidences; take note of that, Olimpio; I would not make a confidant either of you or of anyone else. I am talking about myself to myself, and you are merely giving me the opportunity of doing so. Well then, Olimpio, according to you I am a wicked man who ought to reform, eh?—and, what's more, an unnatural father who ought to turn into a loving one.

OLIMPIO: Not necessarily a loving one, if you don't feel like that. But a just one, certainly.

FRANCESCO: Just—that's a word which sits comfortably on your lips. Just—that is, neither too much this way, nor too much that way; in fact—just. Didn't I tell you you were a reasonable, moderate man? How then could you understand me, who am not, and never was, either moderate or reasonable? Take Beatrice, for instance. Do you know why, when we were on our way up here on horseback and you were throwing little remarks at me from time to time in her defence —do you know why I didn't answer you?

OLIMPIO: You were furious.

FRANCESCO: No, I wasn't furious, I was pleased. I had found the lost thread of my life and was afraid of losing it again, if I went into explanations with you. And this thread was Beatrice's disobedience and the punishment I meant to inflict upon her as soon as possible.

OLIMPIO: I think you ought to be satisfied with keeping her up here for some time longer: it's punishment enough for any disobedience.

FRANCESCO: If I were the just man you would like me to be. But I am not a just man, Olimpio.

OLIMPIO: The devil knows what you are.

FRANCESCO: Aha, yes, the devil indeed. But do a bit of reasoning, Olimpio, seeing how reasonable you are. I know what people say about me in Rome: Francesco Cenci has ruined himself with his vices and can't give his daughter a dowry and that's why he keeps her shut up at La Petrella. So it seems that I'm just a miser, a miserable miser. But don't you see, Olimpio—don't you see the disproportion between my miserliness and Beatrice's imprisonment? Have you not observed that there is what I may call an excess in my behaviour towards Beatrice?

OLIMPIO: Lord Francesco, men judge by common sense. They see that your daughter has done nothing wrong and that in spite of that you are punishing her, and so they think you are doing it from miserliness.

FRANCESCO: Always a motive for everything; motives all the time, Olimpio. However there is a grain of truth in what you say. Beatrice, according to you, has done nothing wrong.

OLIMPIO: And therefore . . . ?

FRANCESCO: Therefore she is innocent.

OLIMPIO: Yes, of course.

FRANCESCO: Oh, how shall I ever make myself understood by a man who is not only reasonable but also entirely devoid of imagination? Don't you see,

Olimpio, that there is a connection between Beatrice's innocence and the excess of punishment that I inflict upon her?

OLIMPIO: Forgive me, but I don't follow you.

FRANCESCO: You needn't follow me; anyhow I'm talking for my own benefit. There is a connection and this connection originates from me and in me, because I am now unable to feel myself alive except through the exercise of cruelty. But you, of course, consider that only the guilty should be punished. You cannot understand that one may prefer to punish the innocent.

OLIMPIO: Punish the innocent?

FRANCESCO: Yes indeed!

OLIMPIO: Lord Francesco, excuse me; please let us leave explanations alone and come to facts.

FRANCESCO: I have done nothing so far except speak of facts, Olimpio.

OLIMPIO: That may be. The facts, anyhow, are these: your daughter disobeyed you in writing that letter to her brother. Punish her, therefore, by prolonging her stay at La Petrella: for her, I can assure you, that is a punishment. But do not punish her otherwise unless you wish to overshoot the mark and show her, as well as me, that you have an interest in punishing her in any case, whether she is guilty or not.

FRANCESCO: And why should I not let her see it? After all, it's the truth.

OLIMPIO: Why? Really you ask questions which are very difficult to answer.

FRANCESCO: I am not a just man, Olimpio, as I've already told you.

OLIMPIO: But do at least be unjust with some moderation.

FRANCESCO: Unjust with moderation? Is it ever possible to be unjust with moderation? Hitherto, with Beatrice, I have been immoderately unjust, and I shall continue to be so in future because things have turned out like that. Should I then—in order to give you pleasure—be reasonably, partially unjust, unjust by halves? No, I shall go to the lowest depths of injustice. In any case it will not be prudence that will stop me; I shall stop only when I am satisfied.

OLIMPIO: What satisfaction can you find in torturing your own daughter?

FRANCESCO: I am made like that, Olimpio, and I cannot change my nature.

OLIMPIO: Lord Francesco, you say that I am reasonable, which indeed is the truth. My reasonableness persuades me, at this point, that it is useless to persist any further with you and that, if I do so, I shall merely show proof that I am not reasonable. So you must do as you please.

FRANCESCO: That is what I decided to do from the very beginning, dearest Olimpio. Good-bye, Olimpio. Till later, then, Olimpio. (*Exit.*)

SCENE 6

Olimpio and Beatrice

BEATRICE: Where is my father?

OLIMPIO: I think he has gone to wash. We have been in the saddle for two days.

BEATRICE: Why has my father come up to the Castle?

OLIMPIO: As far as I know, for no particular reason.

BEATRICE: You are not telling the truth.

OLIMPIO: *You* tell it, then.

BEATRICE: I do not know whether I can trust you. You are one of my father's men and you are Governor of the Castle. If I tell you what I think, I may betray myself and—what is worse—be betrayed by you later.

OLIMPIO: Don't worry, I have never betrayed anyone.

BEATRICE: So say you.

OLIMPIO: Beatrice, do as you please. If you don't trust me, don't speak.

BEATRICE: No, I do trust you, I want to trust you

—or rather, I am compelled to trust you. Tell me, my dear Olimpio, my father didn't mention anything to you about a letter?

OLIMPIO: Ah yes, the letter . . .

BEATRICE: You know about the letter, then, Olimpio? You see, there *was* a reason for this journey of my father's.

OLIMPIO: Forgive me. He mentioned—but very vaguely—some letter or other that you had written. But he did not say that he was coming up here because of the letter.

BEATRICE: He did not say that?

OLIMPIO: No, certainly not.

BEATRICE: I sent this letter secretly, by Marzio, to my brother. In the letter I begged my brother to come and fetch me from here and take me back to Rome. That letter should not have fallen into my father's hands. Why did my father get possession of it, why, Olimpio?

OLIMPIO: Calm yourself, I beg you. Probably it was your brother himself who showed it to your father.

BEATRICE: But I told him not to do so.

OLIMPIO: He must have had reasons of his own.

BEATRICE: But what reasons?

OLIMPIO: How should I know?

BEATRICE: And you maintain that my father did not come up here because of the letter? No—I know him. He read the letter and rushed up here, in a fury, to punish me.

OLIMPIO: Calm yourself, I tell you. During our journey he spoke to me often of you, but he did not say a word about any punishment.

BEATRICE: What did he say about me?

OLIMPIO: He spoke to me about your future.

BEATRICE: About my future? Have I a future?

OLIMPIO: You are twenty years old. Do you not want to have a future?

BEATRICE: And what did he say?

OLIMPIO: I got the impression that your father is forced to do what he is doing because he is not able to do more, or otherwise.

BEATRICE: I do not understand you. I merely feel that there is something unfavourable to myself in what you say—as usual.

OLIMPIO: I will explain at once. As we rode, we got to talking about you; and then your father expounded his reasons to me perfectly clearly. Judge for yourself: your father, last time he was in prison, had to pay a fine of a hundred thousand *scudi*. You are perhaps not unaware that such a sum is extremely difficult to collect together—even if you are called Cenci. Nevertheless, with a supreme effort your father succeeded in scraping this amount together, and so was set at liberty. Now, as you know, your father put down a dowry of twenty thousand *scudi* for your sister Antonina, at the time she was married. But at the present moment, on account of this fine, he does not possess even two thousand *scudi*—let alone twenty thousand. This, therefore, and no other, is the reason why he feels it impossible to find a husband for you. As for the consequences of all this, you can easily imagine them without my needing to explain them.

BEATRICE: The consequences? What consequences?

OLIMPIO: When all's said and done, nothing so terrible. I imagine he will keep you up here at the Castle for some time longer. At any rate until he has put his affairs in order again and once more has the money that would be necessary for your dowry.

BEATRICE: Some time? What does "some time" mean?

OLIMPIO: That I do not know. Perhaps another year, perhaps two years.

BEATRICE: And you have the heart to say: nothing terrible?

OLIMPIO: What can I say? Many people live in fortresses and castles without feeling themselves to be prisoners on that account. Don't I myself live in one? Doesn't my wife do the same? Yet we don't consider ourselves unfortunate.

BEATRICE: But you, Olimpio, you who talk so calmly of keeping me up here for another two years, what do you yourself think of all this?

OLIMPIO: I am not free to disclose my own thoughts in any way, even if, in reality, I have thoughts of my own. I am Governor of the Castle, I am dependent on your father, and I follow out his orders.

BEATRICE: And up till now you have been talking as Governor of the Castle?

OLIMPIO: Yes.

BEATRICE: Dear Olimpio, I beg you now to talk as Olimpio. Tell me, Olimpio, would you do to your daughter Vittoria what my father is doing to me?

OLIMPIO: No, certainly not.

BEATRICE: And why not?

OLIMPIO: Because I am fond of my daughter.

BEATRICE: You wouldn't do it, eh? Then what do you think of my father?

OLIMPIO: Why do you want to know?

BEATRICE: Ah, that I hardly know myself. To get a little comfort, perhaps. My stepmother is a fool, Marzio is a servant, your wife lives outside the Castle, in the village; there's no one else but you here. To whom can I turn except you?

OLIMPIO: Indeed, there's no one else but me. At last you've discovered that.

BEATRICE: I would have spoken to you before, but I was afraid. To me, you were the Governor of the Castle, my father's trusted adjutant.

OLIMPIO: Now, however, it is not the Governor of the Castle but Olimpio who stands face to face with you and speaks to you. Beatrice, if I tell you what I think, you must promise me, in return, not to repeat a word of it to your father.

BEATRICE: And why should I speak of it to my father?

OLIMPIO: One never knows. Women have a way of worming out secrets. And then going, if you please, and saying: "Olimpio thinks the same as I do."

BEATRICE: I will never do that, I promise you.

OLIMPIO: Well, I think your father is one of the wickedest men I have ever known. I think he torments you unjustly. And I think you are worthy of pity because you suffer innocently.

BEATRICE: Thank you, Olimpio.

(*Beatrice presses Olimpio's hand. Olimpio is confused.*)

BEATRICE: Well then, it is as you have said: every-thing comes from the hundred thousand *scudi* that my father had to pay to get out of prison. And that fine of a hundred thousand *scudi* came from his vices. And his vices—where do they come from? From hell.

OLIMPIO: Or from heaven—seeing that everything in this world is decided in heaven.

BEATRICE: Heaven cannot wish an innocent person to be punished, simply for the fact of having been born.

OLIMPIO: Come, calm yourself.

BEATRICE: I cannot calm myself. And so I shall never escape from here—except dead.

OLIMPIO: I did not say that.

BEATRICE: So, while all other girls of my age and position get married and live happily with their husbands and children, I am to languish—for who knows how much longer—in this horrible place, alone, without affection, without family, without life?

OLIMPIO: Please try and calm yourself. The day will certainly come when you will leave here and go back to Rome. It is true that you must not deceive yourself into thinking that this will happen soon; but you must not think, either, that it is never going to happen at all. In the meantime, however, why don't you try and forget the unfavourable sides of your situation and turn your mind to any good which there may be in it?

BEATRICE: Is there anything good here in this place, for me?

OLIMPIO: Yes, there is, if only you would take the trouble to find it.

BEATRICE: I have had almost two years to become aware of it, and I am not aware of it yet.

OLIMPIO: Because your mind goes searching far away from here, in Rome or elsewhere, and you fail to notice that this good thing is really close beside you.

BEATRICE (*sitting down and clasping her head between her hands*): I don't understand, I don't understand. (*She weeps.*)

OLIMPIO (*he looks round and then places his hand on Beatrice's head*): Come, Beatrice, do not weep.

BEATRICE: Forgive me, but I cannot help myself. It is too much for me. If I didn't weep I should scream.

OLIMPIO: You would scream?

BEATRICE (*jumping to her feet and crying out*): Yes, I should scream like this (*she gives a piercing cry and then throws herself, sobbing, into Olimpio's arms*).

OLIMPIO: Enough of those tears, I tell you. And remember that here, in this Castle, if only you wish, you can make things very much better for yourself.

BEATRICE: I don't understand, I don't understand. I have never understood anything, never, since was born. As a little girl, I used to think: I don't understand because I'm only a child. But then I was forced to see that I was wrong: the years went by and still I went on not understanding. I don't understand you, Olimpio.

OLIMPIO: Lift up your head and look at me.

(*Beatrice raises her tear-stained face. Olimpio kisses her on the mouth. Beatrice springs away from him.*)

BEATRICE: Ah, so that was the good thing in store for me, here at the Castle? That! I shall speak to my father about it.

OLIMPIO: Oh no, you will not.

BEATRICE: And why should I not? After all, he is still my father, and I am sure that, when he knows, he will punish you.

OLIMPIO: You will not speak to him, in the first place because you have need of me, since I am the only person here who understands you and is sorry for you. But there is another reason also why you will not speak.

BEATRICE: I do not know what to do with pity like yours.

OLIMPIO: You will not speak because, in actual fact, your father has decided to keep you up here not for a year, or for two years, but for the rest of your days; that is the truth, I swear upon my honour. If your father comes to know that I love you, I shall certainly be forced to leave. And in my place he will appoint some vile and ruthless slave-driver who will make your life intolerable. (*Exit.*)

BEATRICE: For the rest of my days? Olimpio, Olimpio . . .

(*As she seeks to follow Olimpio she runs into her father, who comes in at the same moment.*)

SCENE 7

FRANCESCO: Where were you going? And in such a hurry?

BEATRICE: Let me alone. I was going to my room.

FRANCESCO: Beatrice, it's a month since you've seen your father, and you don't come to meet him, you don't welcome him, you don't embrace him. Shame, Beatrice, shame!

BEATRICE: Why should I welcome you and embrace you—why?

FRANCESCO: Because I am your father, of course.

BEATRICE: As you like: welcome to you, then! And now let me go.

FRANCESCO: Is that all, Beatrice? Is that all? But, Beatrice, that is not the way an affectionate daughter should behave.

BEATRICE: How should an affectionate daughter behave, according to you?

FRANCESCO: She should kiss her father on both cheeks.

(*Beatrice, resigned, advances without a word towards her father. Francesco makes a movement with his hand in order to brush back his hair. Beatrice thinks that her father is intending to strike her, and hides her face with a groan of fear.*)

FRANCESCO: Why, what is this? Are you frightened?

BEATRICE: Yes, you frighten me.

FRANCESCO: Why, Beatrice? Am I so ugly?

BEATRICE: I don't know; I only know that you frighten me.

FRANCESCO: Devil take it, what kind of a fear is this? You should not be frightened except when it is right for you to be frightened. And there is nothing now that need make you afraid. Here am I, with open arms, an affectionate father seeing his daughter again after a long absence. Come, embrace me.

(*Beatrice complies coldly. Francesco thrusts her away.*)

FRANCESCO: Is that your way of embracing me?

BEATRICE: Tell me how I ought to do it.

FRANCESCO: Why, like this—and this! (*He kisses her on both cheeks, noisily, in a humorous manner.*) But I begin to wonder, now, whether this fear of yours may not perhaps have some foundation. Are you frightened of me, or are you frightened because you feel guilty towards me? The distinction is important.

49

BEATRICE: Really I do not know what faults I could be guilty of, up here in this prison.

FRANCESCO: One can be guilty of faults even in a barred cell; don't you know that, Beatrice?

BEATRICE: According to my own conscience, I am not guilty of any faults.

FRANCESCO: According to your conscience? Are you quite sure? Evidently you have a conscience that does not trouble you much. It must be a lazy, sleepy conscience. We must try and rouse it, mustn't we, Beatrice?

BEATRICE: Tell me what you have in mind and let me go.

FRANCESCO: I have nothing in mind. It is your mind, on the contrary, that is burdened with things unexpressed. And I am here to help you unload them. Let us take them in order: you are frightened.

BEATRICE: I am not frightened except of you.

FRANCESCO: No doubt you are frightened of me; I don't dispute that. But, at this moment, you are frightened of me because you feel guilty towards me.

BEATRICE: That is not true.

FRANCESCO: One does not say to one's own father: that is not true. One says: I fear you are mistaken. Isn't that what one ought to say, Beatrice?

BEATRICE: Well, I fear you have always been mistaken about me.

FRANCESCO: We shall see now whether it is true. You know, then, that you are at fault. And that fault consists in disobedience to my wishes.

BEATRICE: I have not disobeyed you.

FRANCESCO: You have disobeyed me. There is double proof that you have disobeyed me—both in the facts and in the manner. Let us begin with the manner. You knew you were disobeying me and therefore you had recourse to a subterfuge.

BEATRICE: I have not had recourse to any subterfuge.

FRANCESCO: You had recourse to a subterfuge, inasmuch as I learned of your disobedience by chance and from third parties. And now let us come to the fact. You wrote a letter to your brother Giacomo. This is the fact.

BEATRICE: I have not written any letter to my brother Giacomo.

FRANCESCO: Here is the letter. Would you like me to read it to you?

BEATRICE: It's no use your reading it, I have not written any letter.

FRANCESCO: You wrote this letter, then, to your brother, and sent it to him by Marzio.

BEATRICE: Marzio is a liar. I did not give him any letter. He says this because you have paid him to say it.

FRANCESCO: Marzio is not a liar and he has not said anything. He handed the letter to your brother, as you had told him to do. Your brother handed it to me.

BEATRICE: Giacomo is a murderer and you and Giacomo came to an agreement and wrote the letter together.

FRANCESCO: This letter is yours, it is written in your handwriting and bears your signature. What is there in this letter, then?

BEATRICE: How should I know, considering that I never wrote it? You can tell me, since it was you who wrote it, you who found it and you who read it.

FRANCESCO: In this letter you beg your brother to fetch you away from the Castle and take you back to Rome.

BEATRICE: That is not true.

FRANCESCO: Ah, then you admit you wrote the letter.

BEATRICE: No, I did not write it, and therefore anything you may assert that it contains is false.

FRANCESCO: You beg your brother to fetch you back to Rome. This is a grave act of disobedience, because I, and I alone, can decide whether to let you go back to Rome or not. I, and no one else. So you are guilty of an initial act of grave disobedience.

BEATRICE: I am not guilty of any act of disobedience.

FRANCESCO: Furthermore, you say in your letter that you desire to get married as soon as possible. This is a second act of grave disobedience. It is not your business to decide when or to whom or in what manner you can get married. It is my business, and mine alone. This is a second act of grave disobedience.

BEATRICE: I have no intention of going into a convent. I wish to get married and have children and to live happily with my husband and my children.

FRANCESCO: Then at least you admit to having written that you wished to find a husband?

BEATRICE: I did not write anything.

FRANCESCO: Finally you conclude by saying that, if it is not arranged for you to be removed from here as soon as possible, you will end by committing some act of folly. What act of folly?

BEATRICE: Would committing a folly also be disobeying you?

FRANCESCO: Certainly it would; the greatest disobedience of all.

BEATRICE: I do not know what you are speaking of.

FRANCESCO: You ought to know, seeing it was you who wrote it. What act of folly?

BEATRICE: It is you who are trying to push me into committing an act of folly. But if there has to be some act of folly, it will certainly be a greater folly than that of writing a letter.

FRANCESCO: What do you mean by that? Are you threatening?

BEATRICE: Yes, but threatening myself. You are trying to force me to kill myself.

FRANCESCO: To kill yourself? And why? What reason have you to kill yourself? Do you lack anything? Are you not content?

BEATRICE: Ah, so I ought to be content?

FRANCESCO: If you were not content, you might have written the letter. But, since you affirm that you did not write it, I presume you are content.

BEATRICE: You are trying to make me confess that I wrote that letter. But I did not write it, and that is the truth.

FRANCESCO: Then you deny everything?

BEATRICE: I have already told you that I do not know what you are speaking of.

(*A long silence ensues.*)

FRANCESCO: Your stubbornness in denying everything, even the evidence, does you harm, my daughter. Feeling yourself to be guilty, you are frightened, and being frightened, you deny. But fear does not help you to understand my real intentions. Just as, a moment ago, when I told you to embrace me you hid your face instead, fearing that I was going to strike you. Having written the letter, you expected your brother to come up here to fetch you and take you back to Rome. This led you to imagine that, whereas your brother would be coming to La Petrella for your good, I could have come only to do you harm. The moment has now arrived, my daughter, to tell you: this is not true.

BEATRICE: It is not true?

FRANCESCO: Did it not occur to you that I might have come to La Petrella with exactly the same intentions as your brother?

BEATRICE: How could I have thought that? You have never even been willing to consider the things which you say I wrote in the letter.

FRANCESCO: You see how mistrustful you are? Even now, at the moment when you are almost ready to give in, you are frightened and will not admit that you wrote that letter. And yet, you silly creature, that is the truth: I had come here in order to grant your desires. In order to fetch you and take you back to Rome.

BEATRICE: Are you telling the truth?

FRANCESCO: God is my witness!

BEATRICE: God is your witness? And am I to believe you?

FRANCESCO: You are at liberty not to believe me, but what good will that do you? If you don't believe me, you will never know the truth. If you do believe me, perhaps you will.

BEATRICE: I should like to believe you. But I am so afraid.

FRANCESCO: It is this fear which, unfortunately, has spoilt everything. If you had not been afraid, you would have admitted writing the letter and I, in return, would have granted the request contained in the letter. But you were frightened, you denied everything, you lied. This being so, what can I do for you? By denying that you wrote the letter, you yourself implicitly admit that all is well with you here and that you do not wish to go away. And I am assenting to your wish. I shall go back at once to Rome, but without you.

BEATRICE: Ah, do not do that, I beg.

FRANCESCO: And why should I not?

BEATRICE: Do not go without me. Take me back to Rome.

FRANCESCO: But consider: I came up here because I was moved by your request and had decided to give you what you desired. But now, seeing that you deny having written the letter, my decision is brought to nothing.

BEATRICE (*throwing herself on her knees in front of her father*): I want to believe you; you have called God to witness and I want to believe you. Yes, I wrote that letter. I wrote it because I was desperate and I was thinking of killing myself and before killing myself I wanted to make one last attempt. Yes, I wrote it.

FRANCESCO: Ah, so you wrote it.

BEATRICE: I wrote it, and it is perfectly true that I begged to be taken away from this prison, to go back to Rome, and to be given in marriage or at least placed in a convent. Yes, it is perfectly true. O my father, now I have told you everything, I have put myself in your hands; have pity upon me, have pity upon your own flesh and blood and take me away from here, for the love of God, away from this living death.

FRANCESCO (*after a moment's silence, in a changed voice*): Ah then, you traitress, you liar, you ingrate, you worthless wretch! You write letters without your father's knowledge and against his wishes; and at last you admit it. There's always some way of getting at the truth: harshness failed to make you confess, but kindness has succeeded. (*Beatrice stares, petrified with horror, at her father.*)

FRANCESCO: But do you know what I said to Olimpio when he told me that one of the serving-maids was complaining of her treatment up here? I said to him: if she complains again, throw her down from the battlements. I don't know who there is to stop me from doing the same with you.

BEATRICE: Now I know you for what you are; you are not my father, you are a miser, an evil man, a murderer! And I am not your daughter. From this moment you have severed the bond of blood that united us. Throw me down from the battlements, then, if you wish! You will be doing a right thing, for you will kill an enemy, not a daughter!

FRANCESCO: Ah-ha—threats? (*He seizes Beatrice by the hair. Beatrice stands still and stares at him.*)

BEATRICE: You will be sorry for all this.

FRANCESCO: I'll be sorry, eh? Oh no, I shall certainly not be sorry. I have never been sorry, and this is not the moment when I shall begin. Perhaps I might have been sorry if I had told you that I had really come to take you back to Rome. In the meantime—since you've mentioned the word prison—I propose that you should form some slight acquaintance with what that word seriously implies. Go to your room and stay there for as long as I shall think proper. A little solitude and fasting will do you good.

BEATRICE: I shall not move from here.

FRANCESCO (*dragging her away*): Indeed you shall.

BEATRICE: I won't go; leave me alone!

FRANCESCO: Go you shall, whether willingly or by force!

(*He goes out, dragging Beatrice with him.*)

SCENE 8

OLIMPIO AND MARZIO

MARZIO: Did you see how he was dragging her along the corridor and at the same time slapping her face and hitting her about the body and shouting all sorts of insults and threats at her?

OLIMPIO: Yes indeed I did; and it made me realize how much I love her, because it made my blood boil. It was only the thought that those blows of his were really furthering my own purpose which held me back. Otherwise I should have leapt upon him, and I might even have killed him.

MARZIO: Are you still convinced, then, that you have been able to keep his fury within the bounds of what is useful to yourself?

OLIMPIO: I am convinced that he is a beast, a man full of wickedness and perversity and who wishes to torment his daughter as much as he pleases, without taking thought for the consequences. But I tell you, Marzio—so much the worse for him. As far as I am concerned, my conscience is quiet.

MARZIO: In your place I shouldn't feel so quiet. Did you not notice that she was neither struggling, nor resisting, nor protesting in any way? She was like a dead woman; she let him do whatever he wanted. To me, this passive attitude on her part forebodes no good. As I have already said: you want the daughter to hate her father, but only just enough to make her fall into your arms; and you want the father to ill-treat the daughter, but only just enough to drive her towards you. But the father has already overstepped the mark and I fear the daughter is on the point of doing the same thing.

OLIMPIO: You always foresee the worst.

MARZIO: No; but I warned you—despair is a bad ally. And the daughter is cast in the same mould as her father. Just as the father is extravagant in his perversity, so is she in her innocence.

OLIMPIO: Bah, perversity may possibly be dangerous, but innocence can never be so.

MARZIO: Mark my words, Olimpio, what you are looking for is a prudent kind of innocence. But don't you know that innocence is the one thing that knows no moderation?

SCENE 9

OLYMPIO, MARZIO AND LUCREZIA

LUCREZIA: What has been happening? I heard shouts, and the sound of blows, and moaning; and I rushed out and ran into Francesco as he came out of Beatrice's room panting and with his face all distorted; and he pushed me aside and almost knocked me down. Then I went into the room and found Beatrice lying there bleeding and bruised, in a faint. But she came to almost at once and threw her arms round my neck and kept on sobbing and saying: "Tell me I'm not his daughter. Tell me my mother deceived him with one of the grooms. Tell me, for God's sake, that he's not my father." Then she fainted again. I could not lift her up from the floor by myself, so I came to ask you to come and help me lay her on the bed.

OLIMPIO: Best leave her where she is. Why try to interfere between her and Lord Francesco? She'll come to by herself, no fear.

LUCREZIA: You too have no heart—like Francesco.

You should have seen her—her face covered with blood, her clothes torn. And what has she done wrong? I ask you—what crime has she committed?

OLIMPIO: Ah, leave us in peace! But look . . . here she comes.

SCENE 10

OLIMPIO, MARZIO, LUCREZIA AND BEATRICE

BEATRICE: Marzio, Lucrezia, I call you to witness. A little time ago this man, although he is the Governor of this Castle and is bound by solemn duty towards all who live in it, and is a husband and father, this man made me proffers of love. And I repulsed him and even threatened to tell my father. But it was the old Beatrice who then resisted and threatened him. The new one will not do so.

OLIMPIO: Be silent! You are ill, you speak as if you were delirious.

BEATRICE: But I wish there to be no deceit, no illusions, in what is about to happen. Olimpio, I know now that you have been calculating upon my despair in order to get possession of me. That possession you shall have, but I am no longer desperate now and my giving myself to you will not be the end of my despair, as perhaps you thought, but the beginning of something else. (*Exit.*)

MARZIO: You see, Olimpio, was I not right? You will get altogether more than you hoped for.

LUCREZIA: O Lord, have pity! How could you do this, Olimpio—you of all people—with a defenceless creature like Beatrice? And I, what am I to do now? If I were to tell Francesco, he is capable of actually killing her.

OLIMPIO: You must do nothing. I take upon myself everything that is going to happen. And you, Marzio, you may be sure that I shall get exactly as much as I wanted, not more. We all seek to justify ourselves. She can give what name she likes to what she is going to do. But it will still be the love that she has need of. And when love is established, all else will cease and there will be only love.

ACT TWO

SCENE 1

(*The main room at the Castle of La Petrella. The windows are wide open. It is summer.*)

OLIMPIO: What is all this about? You want to go away? And why?

MARZIO: Because I find life altogether too easy up here at La Petrella. I am afraid of becoming enfeebled with so many entertainments and pleasures.

OLIMPIO: What do you mean? You are always playing the buffoon and one never knows when you are speaking seriously.

MARZIO: I play the buffoon, as you say, in self-defence. What does the cuttlefish do when it is attacked? It envelops itself in its own ink and disappears. I do likewise: I try to envelop myself and disappear in the midst of what you call my buffooneries.

OLIMPIO: Come now, tell me—why do you want to go away?

MARZIO: I have already told you: because life is too pleasant. Who indeed would not find life pleasant up here? Clear, pure mountain air with a touch of sharpness in it. We go early to bed—especially you, Olimpio, though it's in a bed that isn't your own; and we rise very early indeed, as you know yourself, when you go off to your house in the first glimmer of dawn. Besides, Lord Francesco keeps us all cheerful with his pranks and caprices; he can be said to invent a new one every single day. He makes the servant-girls go bare-footed and almost naked, it is true; but he does this, not from miserliness, but to cheer us with a sight of feminine nudity. It is also true that he beats his wife and daughter, good and hard; but this again is not done from unkindness but merely to enliven us: those concerts of shrieks and groans, of mutterings and cursings, are truly delightful to the ear. And, I assure you, it's enough to make anyone burst with laughter to see Lord Francesco drag up the close-stool near the fire and sit on it in nothing but his shirt and do his business and then call his daughter and order her: "Come on, Beatrice, come and give me a real good wipe . . ." And it's really a highly amusing sight to see Lady Beatrice, as she cleans him up, turning away her head and trying to avoid both seeing and smelling. And again, who could help laughing at the sight of Lord Francesco when he lies down naked on the bed in the evening and makes his daughter scratch him where he has the itch? He says to her: "Come along, scratch, scratch, harder, harder, higher up now, scratch, scratch"; and she scratches away as hard as she can, with both hands, making all the time the most comic grimaces of disgust! There's plenty to laugh at at meals, too, when Lord Francesco, at each course, pushes the dish towards his daughter and says: "Come, my sweet Beatrice, act as taster for me. There might be poison in it." Oh yes, Signor Olimpio, in such circumstances who could fail to be amused?

OLIMPIO: There is nothing new in all this. It used to happen even a year, or two years, ago. What new thing is there that makes you want to leave?

MARZIO: Do you wish me to speak frankly?

OLIMPIO: Certainly.

MARZIO: Well, you remember what I said to you some months ago, that time when you arrived from Rome with Lord Francesco and told me that Lady Beatrice's despair was your best ally. I said to you: be careful, despair is a bad ally and you will find yourself getting a good deal more than you want.

OLIMPIO: Well, then?

MARZIO: Well, then, what I feared has happened. By insisting that the letter she wrote to her brother should be handed to her father, you have unleashed Lady Beatrice's despair. And, as you had rightly foreseen, Lady Beatrice, because of her despair, has given

69

herself to you. At that point you thought to stop her. But she has not stopped. What for you was the end—in other words, love—was, for her, merely a means. What for you was the fulfilment was, for her, the beginning. You set a trap, but you yourself were the first to put your foot in it; you constructed a machine and now your machine is overwhelming you.

OLIMPIO: Even allowing that this is true—which it is not—I ask you once again: why do you want to go away?

MARZIO: Because I am afraid.

OLIMPIO: Afraid of what?

MARZIO: Afraid of you and Lady Beatrice; but, above all, afraid of myself.

OLIMPIO: You must be the only person in the world to be afraid of Marzio!

MARZIO: I do not want to be misunderstood. I know quite well that I am not a violent man. I am not the kind of man who looks at his own hands and trembles at the thought of what they might be capable of doing on certain occasions. But I am poor, and being poor I am covetous. What others do from violence, I might do from covetousness. I began to be afraid of myself on the day when you told me you had been to visit Lady Beatrice in her room.

OLIMPIO: What have you to do with that?

MARZIO: I have already had something to do with it. And I can tell you how. Some time ago, finding myself alone with Lady Beatrice, I made mention of the difficulties in which I find myself, with a wife and four children to feed on nothing but a few tunes on the guitar. And, almost in spite of myself, I hinted that I knew a number of things and that, some day or other, my difficulties might suggest my making use of the things I knew. One moment earlier I had not thought of this, mind you; and it is just this that makes me afraid—this lack of premeditation, this spontaneity. Lady Beatrice naturally showed understanding of my troubles. She took ten *scudi* out of her purse and gave them to me, and I promised that, so far as I was concerned, no one would ever get to know anything. So, you see, I have already had something to do with it.

OLIMPIO: Blackmail? Beatrice did very wrong to give you those ten *scudi*.

MARZIO: Blackmail! Lord have mercy! No, a thousand times no! A kind of complicity, if anything, which—mind you—I would much prefer to do without but which I seem to be drawn into against my will, by some irresistible means. So far is it from being blackmail that I am in fact asking your permission to go away.

OLIMPIO: Well and good; you know that Beatrice and I love each other, you have been given money not to speak of it, and that's the end of that. Why go away?

MARZIO: But I've already told you, I'm afraid of myself. I know myself and, above all, I know the wretchedness of my family. Do you know that my children go barefoot and half naked? That in my house we have only one meal a day, and often not even that? That my wife is so worn out that she has no milk for the youngest child? When I go home in the evening and see them all looking at me with hungry eyes, I feel that, for their sake, I might easily commit a crime. I know myself, I tell you, and I know for certain that, the more I get to know, the more I shall ask for, and, the more I ask for, the more deeply I shall become involved.

OLIMPIO: Involved in what?

MARZIO: Alas, I do not know, though at moments I can suspect it. And it is because of that, too, that I am afraid.

OLIMPIO: You asked my leave to speak frankly. But you have not done so.

MARZIO: I have told you everything.

OLIMPIO: No, you have not told everything. And— to speak really frankly—you are not afraid and you do not wish to go.

MARZIO: May I die if it is not true!

OLIMPIO: Oh yes, it is true; but perhaps at the same

time it is not true. And in fact, if I said to you: "Go",
you would be much disappointed. You do not want
to go away, you do want to know. And, in asking
to be allowed to go, you are expressing, not so much
fear, as spite at not knowing. And you desire to know,
because you imagine that if you know you will be
able to ask for more. Perhaps you are really afraid
of becoming involved. But your covetousness is
stronger than your fear. You want to know: well,
I will satisfy your curiosity.

MARZIO: You will satisfy my curiosity?

OLIMPIO: Yes, since you wish it. I know I am expos-
ing myself to possible blackmail. But I want to take
you at your word and to believe that between us two
there will never be blackmail but only complicity.

MARZIO: One moment, please; no, don't tell me
anything. Be strong on my behalf and do not lead me
into temptation. Don't tell me anything, and I will
go away and come back when all is over.

OLIMPIO: What is it now? Are you really, perchance,
more frightened than covetous?

MARZIO: No, I am certainly—as you said—more
covetous than frightened. But do, I beg you, do behave
as if I were more frightened than covetous.

OLIMPIO: Briefly then—do you want to know or not
to know? Do you want to stay here or to go away?
Do you want to acquire or to renounce?

MARZIO: As God is my witness, I do not know myself what I want. I put myself in your hands.

OLIMPIO: You put yourself in my hands? But I cannot do more than think of myself.

MARZIO: For once, think of me. Ask yourself: is it right that poor Marzio should know certain things? But be careful; make sure it is the Marzio who is at the same time both covetous and frightened, who has a family that is dying of hunger, who plays the guitar. Not just any Marzio, but that particular one.

OLIMPIO: I have already told you, I cannot do more than think of myself. And, after weighing the pros and cons, I consider it suits me better that you should know. Possibly, if you did not already know about our love affair, I might have been able to leave you in ignorance. But you know the tie that binds me to Beatrice, and so, if anything happens, you might betray us—even without meaning to—by revealing the little you do know. But, if you know everything, you will be able, in fact you will have, to deny everything. And so, whether you wish it or not, you have to know.

MARZIO: Do I have to know at once?

OLIMPIO: Yes.

MARZIO: This very moment? Without any time to think things over? Why not tomorrow, for instance?

OLIMPIO: No, at once.

MARZIO: As you wish.

OLIMPIO: Well, know then: by this time Lord Francesco is already dead.

MARZIO: Mercy! God have pity upon us! It's not possible!

OLIMPIO: So possible is it that it has already happened.

MARZIO: Dead? Lord Francesco dead?

OLIMPIO: Yes, at least an hour ago.

MARZIO: Ah, I suspected all the time that this would happen and now I know it for certain. And how can I manage now not to know it, if I want to be ignorant of it? Ah, you've told me and I know and there's nothing to be done about it; poor Marzio, there's nothing to be done about it.

OLIMPIO: For once you speak the truth: there's nothing to be done about it.

MARZIO: Did you kill him? They'll discover us and I who am guiltless will be involved in it, and no one will believe that I am guiltless. Poor Marzio, this is the end of you.

OLIMPIO: Keep calm and do not be so frightened. They won't discover us and you will not be involved. And anyhow, *I* haven't killed him.

MARZIO: Then he's still alive?

OLIMPIO: No, he is dead. But let me tell you every-thing; and you will see that you don't need to have any more fear. I wish you to know that I have done everything with great caution, in such a way that no one can be blamed for his death—I mean no one of us here at the Castle. Because the whole thing had to be done with circumspection, seeing that it was a question, after all, of Lord Francesco Cenci and not of some ordinary poor man. I worked out a plan, therefore, which by this time, according to my calcula-tions, should have been already carried out.

MARZIO: You say that Lord Francesco is already dead?

OLIMPIO: Certainly he is.

MARZIO: Then do not tell me any more. Nothing more that you can tell me will have the weight of what you have already said.

OLIMPIO: No, I want you to be reassured.

MARZIO: Or rather, you want to reassure yourself?

OLIMPIO: I was never so sure of myself as I am now. Well then, I found myself faced with a difficult problem—to do the thing in such a way that not merely should it not be attributed to us, but that it should also seem to have been done for a motive other than the real one. I thought about it for a long time and in the end it seemed to me that I had found a solution. As you know, there are a number of bandits

living in the mountains about here—men who have
gone into hiding in order to escape justice. The largest
of these bands of brigands is at Marcetello, not far
from here, and it so happens that I know their chief
very well, because he was a soldier with me in Prince
Colonna's army at Lepanto. So, one day recently,
pretending that I was going out hunting, I went all
the way to Marcetello and found this brigand chief
and made him this proposal: I told him that Lord
Francesco has a habit of riding in the hills on horseback, and that he must waylay him and attack him
and, on some pretext or other, kill him. For you, I
said to him, this will be just one more murder; not
doing it certainly won't save you from the galleys,
nor will doing it increase the punishment that's in
store for you. We talked it over for a bit and finally
came to an agreement, and the same day I sent him
half the sum I had promised him. The other half he
will receive when it's all over. Tomorrow, in other
words; for today was the day fixed.

MARZIO: But today Lord Francesco has gone out
riding with Beatrice. Have you had the father killed
under the very eyes of the daughter?

OLIMPIO: Beatrice knows of it and agreed to it.

MARZIO: Agreed to it?

OLIMPIO: Yes, we were in agreement from the very
beginning.

MARZIO: Now, tell me the truth: it was she who suggested it, who asked you to do it, who *made* you do it.

OLIMPIO: What does it matter who was the first to think of it? We were in agreement, that's all.

MARZIO: No, it matters very much. Ah, I recognize you in this again, Olimpio, I recognize you. You are reasonable and you are vain and you think that everything can be done as it is in the kitchen, with recipes and measured portions, and at the same time you try to deceive yourself into imagining that everything depends upon you and that nothing slips through your fingers. Vain and reasonable, that is what you are.

OLIMPIO: But what is troubling you now? The important thing was to achieve a particular purpose.

MARZIO: Perhaps; but her purpose, Beatrice's purpose, not yours. Yours, alas, you have not achieved, nor will you ever achieve it. Some time ago you were under the illusion that you could keep Beatrice in check by means of a love affair. But you have not checked her. Now you are deceiving yourself that this crime will check her, imagining that a daughter can kill her father and still remain just as she was before. But I tell you, you will not achieve your purpose this time either. And I also tell you that it is she who holds the reins, not you. And once again I repeat, you have constructed a machine which will overwhelm you.

Would I had never known! Which will overwhelm us both.

OLIMPIO: I could not refuse. It is one thing to have a request made to you by someone who means nothing to you, in ordinary surroundings; another, when the request comes from your own mistress, in the depths of the night, at the moment of abandonment when her body and yours are one.

MARZIO: Oh, how you are deceived! Tell me, what do you think was her motive when she opened the door of her room to you?

OLIMPIO: That is a question of honour, and I am a man of honour and a soldier. I don't wish to speak to you about it.

MARZIO: You are a soldier, oh yes, you're a real soldier, and like all soldiers you are both easy-going and obtuse and think that things can be done by cleverness and by force and can be brought to a stop just when you like, like military manoeuvres. You want to deceive yourself into thinking that you have carried out a brilliant manoeuvre—isn't that right? Whereas you don't realize that you have been led by the nose the whole time. And so, what do you think Beatrice's motive was, in giving herself to you? Was it for your fine upstanding figure? Or because of your glorious past? Or because of the wounds you suffered at Lepanto?

79

OLIMPIO: Oh, enough, that's enough now.

MARZIO: But why do you want to make me believe you didn't know that Beatrice was making use of you to take vengeance on her father? Why in the world do you try and make me think you were unaware that she gave herself to you on the tacit understanding that you, in return, would help her to get rid of her father?

OLIMPIO: Enough, I tell you.

MARZIO: Ah, if all that was needed was to say "enough", perhaps you would be right. But that, alas, is not so.

OLIMPIO: I may be nothing more than a soldier and understand nothing except manoeuvres. But the only thing you can do is to talk, and talking never led to anything.

MARZIO: Are you quite sure about all this?

OLIMPIO: I do not see what else can happen; nor why in the world, once her father is dead, I should still keep Beatrice in check. At what point, and why? We were forced to rid ourselves of her father, and now we have done so and are free at last to decide on our own lives, just this. From now onwards everything will be clearer, easier and more just.

MARZIO: Yes. And so they lived happily ever afterwards.

OLIMPIO: The truth is that you are afraid.

MARZIO: Yes, I am afraid. If men were machines or even perhaps soldiers, you might be right. But it is not so; and I am afraid.

OLIMPIO: You should trust me and not think of other things. (*Exit.*)

SCENE 2

MARZIO AND LUCREZIA

(*Marzio tunes his guitar and starts playing.*)

LUCREZIA: Was not Olimpio here?

MARZIO: Yes, he was, but he has gone.

LUCREZIA: I want to speak to Olimpio. But he knows I want to speak to him and he avoids me.

MARZIO: Why ever should you think he avoids you?

LUCREZIA: Because he means to pursue his own pleasure, exactly as he wishes, and is indifferent to what happens to others—in fact does not even wish to know about it. And yet we ourselves are not the only people in the world; there are others as well. A little understanding and a little charity would not come amiss.

MARZIO: By "others" you mean yourself, eh?

LUCREZIA: Of course; does that surprise you? *I* am in the world too. Beatrice and Olimpio, on the other hand, behave as though I were not. It is impossible for all this to go on as it is at present, quite impossible.

MARZIO: All this?

LUCREZIA: Don't pretend not to understand me. When Beatrice and I were alone up here and shut up as if in prison, I used sometimes to think to myself: it can never be worse than this; whatever happens, it is bound to be better. But I was wrong. Something worse has happened.

MARZIO: The worst has yet to happen.

LUCREZIA: What, in your opinion, could be worse? A virtuous girl, who ought to have been married and to have lived quietly with her husband and children, has become the strumpet of a rough, vulgar, common man, inferior to herself both in rank and breeding, and, into the bargain, much older than herself and a married man and the father of three children. Could anything possibly be worse than this?

MARZIO: I do not know. But in any case I do not see what harm this does to you. Beatrice, by becoming, as you say, Olimpio's strumpet, has injured only herself.

LUCREZIA: It is me she has injured more than anyone. She desired this, and Olimpio desired it, and so they have thrown honour to the winds and every night they take their pleasure together. What harm has Beatrice done to herself, in so far as she has renounced honour for love's sake? No harm at all; in fact, a great deal of good, I think, if it is true—

as indeed it *is* true—that love repays any sacrifice whatsoever.

MARZIO: *You* know that—eh?

LUCREZIA: I too have been young and I too have loved. I tell you, Marzio, it is to me the harm has been done. While they are embracing in the room next door, and kissing and hugging and biting as lovers do, my heart is in my mouth all night long, in terror lest Lord Francesco, sleeping beside me, should hear something and get to know of their passion. Twice already he has heard Olimpio walking on tiptoe along the passage or opening Beatrice's door; he wanted to get up and go and look, and I had to dissuade him, telling him it was mice or the wind. Once someone sneezed in the passage and he woke up crying: "Who's there?" So I pretended I had to leave the room for the needs of nature, and there they were, the two of them, in the passage, and although I begged them to go away they paid no attention to me but stayed there fondling and embracing each other quite at their ease, and Beatrice was naked as her mother bore her, and I had to watch this pretty love scene when all the time I was dying of fright, in terror that the door would open and *he* appear on the threshold. And if it were only the nights! But they seem to make a particular point of defying danger in the daytime too, especially Beatrice, who, at meals, sits all the time with one hand above the table and the other underneath it squeezing Olimpio's hand. Or, if her father turns away for a moment, she plants a kiss on Olimpio's cheek or gives him some other mark of affection. And all the time I am terrified and I sit holding my breath; and if—which God forbid!—he came to know about it, I would be the first person upon whom he would vent his anger. I think he would kill me.

MARZIO: No fear of that; your husband will never come to know.

LUCREZIA: So say you.

MARZIO: Yes, so say I. And, what is more, I tell you that you need have no further fear of him because perhaps at this moment he is no longer able to inspire fear in anyone.

LUCREZIA: You do not know him, Marzio, as I know him.

MARZIO: I knew him too, and I was afraid of him too. But he has become, at this moment, no more to be feared than a scarecrow standing in the middle of a cornfield. From some way off it looks like a real man, but if you approach you discover it's nothing more than a dummy. So it is with your husband.

LUCREZIA: What do you mean?

MARZIO: Are not the dead like scarecrows? They are just like men, except that they have no life. And a man who in life was terrible becomes, when dead, more harmless than the most harmless of living men. Julius Caesar dead inspires less fear than the most wretched of living beggars.

LUCREZIA: I do not understand you.

MARZIO: Comfort yourself, from now onwards you can sleep peacefully.

LUCREZIA: You talk as though my husband were dead!

MARZIO: He is dead indeed. That is just what I am trying to make you understand.

LUCREZIA: My husband—dead? Dead?

MARZIO: Yes, dead, without mercy and without remedy, dead in truth. This morning he went out riding with Beatrice. Olimpio and Beatrice had come to an understanding with the brigands at Marcetello that they should kill him. By this time, as I told you, he is dead.

LUCREZIA: Oh, do not say that, it is too terrible. Poor Francesco! Ah, I knew they were weaving some plot. Ah, how terrible, how terrible! Woe is me!

MARZIO: Do not cry so loud. There is no one here but me. Whom do you wish to hear you?

LUCREZIA: Dead—Francesco—he is dead?

MARZIO: Yes, you must persuade yourself of that. If you repeat it often enough you will end by believing it.

LUCREZIA: I know you do not believe in my grief; I did not love him, it is true, but that does not mean I do not grieve over his loss. Do you really think everything is so simple? Yes, indeed I grieve, and everything seems to me even more terrible than before, and his death adds yet another shadow to my life. Beatrice Olimpio's strumpet and her father's murderess; my husband dead; all life darkened and laid waste: ah no, you do not understand what all this means.

MARZIO: I understand that in a few days' time you will be leaving for Rome with Beatrice and Olimpio. And that there you will come into possession of an inheritance that will make you the richest widow in Rome. And that, in spite of your life being darkened and laid waste, you will live much more happily than before.

LUCREZIA: I have an easy conscience; I knew nothing and I did nothing. For me it is truly as though he had been killed by brigands.

MARZIO: Now you are becoming more reasonable.

LUCREZIA: I am innocent of his death.

MARZIO: No one is accusing you.

LUCREZIA: But I do not wish ever to hear anything more about his death—I mean about the real reasons which brought it about. Neither you, nor Beatrice, nor Olimpio must ever speak to me of it. I know nothing of it. For me it was the bandits who killed him. Remember that.

MARZIO: You must give Beatrice and Olimpio your instructions on that point. I myself knew nothing about it until a moment ago. And yet, unfortunately, to know about it is to be implicated.

LUCREZIA: Not for me.

MARZIO: Then you wish to denounce them?

LUCREZIA: I don't wish anything; oh, leave me alone, I don't wish anything. I could wish he were not dead, but now that he is dead I no longer wish anything. My only wish is to leave this dreadful Castle, to go back to Rome and there to creep into my little corner of life and neither to know nor to hear anything more. Ah, if only I could do as certain animals do! When winter comes, they dig themselves a deep hole and go to sleep in it and don't wake up until spring, and meanwhile they lie hidden away, knowing nothing of the snow and the cold, of night and day. Yes, Marzio, I swear I would like to sleep now for some years and then wake up and be told that it is all over and that I can now live peacefully.

MARZIO: Calm yourself; Olimpio assured me that no one will ever know anything of it.

LUCREZIA: I still cannot believe it. Poor, poor Francesco!

SCENE 3

MARZIO, FRANCESCO AND LUCREZIA

(*Enter Francesco, in riding dress.*)

FRANCESCO (*throwing down his cloak*): Lucrezia, quickly now—go and tell them to serve the meal as quickly as possible. I'm dying of hunger. Eh, Lucrezia, I'm speaking to you!

LUCREZIA (*after a moment's astonishment, jumping to her feet and throwing her arms about her husband's neck*): But you're alive, my husband! My dear husband, you're alive!

FRANCESCO: What's the matter with you? Of course I'm alive, and hungry into the bargain. Come, what are these affectations?

LUCREZIA: You are alive. I have been so afraid you might be dead.

FRANCESCO: What is all this? Dead? Dead tired, perhaps, since we've been riding in the mountains for four hours. But more alive than ever. Now please leave me alone; and—what *is* the matter, I beg you?

LUCREZIA: Let me embrace you. You are alive, after all. He's alive, Marzio!

MARZIO: Indeed he is very much alive.

FRANCESCO: Upon my word, you seem to be crazy, the pair of you. What madness is this? Why should I be dead?

MARZIO: Really, I don't know why.

LUCREZIA: Forgive me. But last night I had a horrible dream which greatly disturbed me. I thought I saw you riding along a mountain path, in winter, in the direction of Marcetello, where there is that band of brigands. And then, all of a sudden, from behind a rock came the explosion of an arquebus and you fell off your horse on to the snow and the snow was all red with your blood and you lay on the path, lifeless and still. I had not the courage to tell you about it this morning, but all the time I was tormenting myself because of the dream, and when I saw you come in I almost thought you were the ghost of yourself. And I wanted to embrace you so as to feel with my own hands that it was really you, in flesh and blood.

FRANCESCO: What a queer kind of dream! Perhaps you wanted it to be like that—eh, Lucrezia? But you can undeceive yourself: I am alive and shall be yet for a long time, so please God.

MARZIO: Yes indeed, for as long as it pleases God.

LUCREZIA: I desire that you may live a long time yet. I dreamt that dream because some days ago we were speaking of the bandits of Marcetello.

FRANCESCO: Yes, but I also told you that those bandits had wished to place themselves under my protection, requesting the favour of being allowed to remain upon my land. You dreamt the opposite of the true state of affairs: what does that mean, Lucrezia?

LUCREZIA: It means that I love you dearly.

FRANCESCO: Enough, enough, I am alive—very much alive, in fact. And my life at this moment is chiefly concerned with my hunger. Go quickly and tell them to hasten with their serving.

LUCREZIA: Yes, yes, I will go.

FRANCESCO: Come with me, Marzio: you shall play to me while I change my clothes. (*Exeunt omnes.*)

SCENE 4

Olimpio and Beatrice

Olimpio: Truly I cannot understand how this can have happened. We were all agreed, and I had paid half of the sum promised; and again yesterday I received assurances about it from one of the band who had come to the village to buy bread. I do not understand.

Beatrice: It is your fate not to understand. If you understood, you would not trust so much to your plans and you would look, rather, to the men who are concerned in those plans. Do you not know that one can never trust anyone but oneself? Not only that; but others, even when they are doing things you want them to do, may still have different aims from your own. You wanted someone killed but the bandits wanted money. When they had thought it over, they decided to be satisfied with half the amount, inasmuch as the other half might cost them a relentless persecution and possibly death. And so they went away.

Olimpio: They went away?

BEATRICE: Yes, they went away. We went all the way to the place where they had their huts, at Marce-tello: and there was nothing left but the low stone walls, which were still smoking. Last night they set fire to the whole place and went away.

OLIMPIO: Gone away.

BEATRICE: Yes, gone away. And a shepherd who was rummaging amongst the ruins, hoping, I suppose, to find something there, told us that they had gone in the direction of the Kingdom of Naples. By this time they must be a long way off.

OLIMPIO: Gone away! Ah, the dogs, the robbers, the murderers! I befriended and helped and protected them, and this is their gratitude.

BEATRICE: Come, they didn't owe you any gratitude. Especially as you had made up your mind to pay them only the first half of the amount, and perhaps they guessed it. Besides, who expects gratitude from bandits?

OLIMPIO: The chief trouble is that we had only that much money and no more. Now we have nothing left. And without money what is to be done?

BEATRICE: That is what I am wondering too.

OLIMPIO: I adopted this plan because it was certain to succeed and was at the same time perfectly ambiguous. No one could have suspected that we were behind the bandits. The bandits, for their part, had enough crimes on their consciences to be able to take this one upon themselves too: what did one more or less matter? And if they had been caught, even if they had revealed the truth, who would have believed them? No one believes bandits.

BEATRICE: You believed them.

OLIMPIO: I could not help doing so, if I wanted the plan to succeed. There was the risk of betrayal, as there always is in such cases. But I had to face that. Now, however, apart from having no more money, we no longer have any plan that is good enough.

BEATRICE: Are you taking great trouble to find a plan that is good?

OLIMPIO: Yes, and I do not wish to try anything which does not hold out a sound probability of success. The first condition of success for a plan of this kind is that it should have two different faces, one for us who carry it through and the other for those who do not take part in it. The first can be the face of guilt itself; but the second must, in all cases, be that of innocence. It was with great difficulty that I worked out this two-faced plan with the bandits. Now really I do not know what more I can devise—for some time at any rate.

BEATRICE: What do you mean to do, then?

OLIMPIO: I think we must wait for another opportunity in the near future. As things now stand, we can wait without impatience and without fear. Nothing forces us to hurry because your father has noticed nothing; in fact, as the days pass, he seems to have less and less suspicion of any kind. He has now settled down into the life here as if it were a bed where sleep was easy. He torments you, it is true, as he has always done; but by some strange illusion he imagines at the same time that he loves you and is loved by you. With me he is extremely affectionate; he cannot do without me. In short—like all those who offend frequently and without reason—he forgets how greatly he has offended. We must wait patiently, calmly, resolutely, our minds in readiness for the next favourable opportunity.

BEATRICE: How long shall we have to wait?

OLIMPIO: That we cannot know precisely. The favourable opportunity might present itself tomorrow: or it might be a month, or a year. We must not be in a hurry. And, if it is true that the present situation is agreeable to your father and that he is unlikely to do anything to change it, we two, on our side, also have good reason not to consider it entirely unfavourable. We have come together, Beatrice, and we love one another and I come to see you every night; in short, we are now in a position to wait without hastening matters unduly. For my part, I would wait for ever.

BEATRICE: There! At last you are being sincere.

OLIMPIO: I say that because I love you. A lover's aim is to love and to be loved, and if he loves and is loved in return he cannot help longing for that to go on for ever.

BEATRICE: So you are hoping, then, that this will go on for ever. But it is not love that inspires this hope in you.

OLIMPIO: I do not see what else it can be.

BEATRICE: A moment ago you said that my father has settled down into the present situation as if it were a comfortable bed where sleep was easy. As for you yourself, you have gone completely off to sleep in that same bed.

OLIMPIO: What do you mean?

BEATRICE: The reason why you want nothing to change is because the situation in which you find yourself really and truly is like a comfortable bed, with plenty of warm blankets well tucked in. On the one hand you have a wife who cooks your food, keeps your house clean, looks after your children and does not enquire where you are going when you leave home in the evening; on the other, a girl of twenty who awaits you in her bed every night, a girl who is the daughter of Francesco Cenci and who sacrifices her honour and degrades her rank on your account. In addition you are Governor of the Castle, a man of high authority, cherished by Francesco Cenci (who suspects nothing; that is agreeable too, eh?) and respected by all. In very truth, who would not wish to prolong for ever a situation like this—so full of delights with so few risks, so very reasonable?

OLIMPIO: But, my love, you say these things to me?

BEATRICE: You claim that you love me, but really it is yourself you love. And at bottom you are not so very different from my father: you too wish to drive me to despair, to torment me, to make me do some foolish thing.

OLIMPIO: But if this were so, my love—reflect a moment: if this were so, I should never have made an agreement with the bandits.

BEATRICE: And how am I to know that you ever did so? Or at least that you made the agreement you say? What can I know of your relations with the bandits? You yourself say you befriended them in so many ways. In return, they might very well have counterfeited the whole thing, in order to please you.

OLIMPIO: You do not know what you are saying. But I do not wish to follow you along this path of rage and suspicion; there, you will always get the better of me.

BEATRICE: You cannot follow me, for, if you did, you would be compelled to admit the truth.

OLIMPIO: But what truth?

BEATRICE: The truth: that you wish things to remain as they are. Some day, in a year, in two years, my father will at last decide to remove me from here and take me back to Rome. And you—at first you will show a certain sadness at so cruel a parting; and then you will think to yourself that all is well that ends well; and you will say to yourself; that little Cenci girl helped me to pass these last two years not too badly, after all. And I shall return to Rome a very different person from what I was when I left it: bereft of honour, of hope, and of love.

OLIMPIO: But, my love, that is not true!

BEATRICE: Oh, do not call me "my love"! Do you think I don't see through your little game?

OLIMPIO: What game? What do you mean?

BEATRICE: You want to wear me down and bring me gradually to accept things as they are. But what ever do you think was the reason why I gave you the keys of my room that night?

OLIMPIO: I thought you loved me.

BEATRICE: I have never talked of love. You have a bad memory. And I wish to recall to you what happened that night, so that you may not again suggest that I should go on waiting. I was wide awake that

night, sitting up in my bed, when you came. A short
time before, I had said my prayers for the last time,
and as I prayed I said to God: henceforward I shall
not pray to You any more because for me it would
be a sacrilege; and the reason for that is that I shall
not be the same person as before, inasmuch as, in order
to bring death to my father, I am first of all bringing
death to myself. And then you came in like a thief,
and crept over to my bed, and I was trembling inside
myself, not so much for what I was about to do as
for what would follow it. You undressed in the dark
and then you came into bed beside me, and at once
you placed your hand on my breast, as if to reassure
yourself that I was now yours. Then I took your hand
and said: "If you love me, you must help me to make
my father regret what he did to me today." And you
said: "I promise anything you wish." And I insisted:
"You must swear that you will help me even if I ask
you to kill him." And then you uttered some terrible
curse, and you seized me violently by the hair and
thrust my head back and, bending down to my open
mouth, you hurled into it the oath I demanded of you,
and then you kissed me hard as though to seal up my
mouth after you had hurled the oath into it. And then
I surrendered myself to you simply because you had
sworn the oath and because I trusted you. But now
that you have got what you desired, you draw back.
Are these, then, your oaths?

OLIMPIO: Certainly I swore that oath, and it is not my intention to draw back. But I do not wish to hasten things unduly, as I said; I wish to take time to prepare a new plan that will give me a guaranteed certainty of success, and I wish to wait for the most favourable moment possible for putting it into effect. We must think of the future, Beatrice, and not only of the near but of the more distant future. That is what you do not think of; you wish to throw yourself into vengeance without troubling to find out whether it may not overwhelm you together with your father.

BEATRICE: I have no future. I destroyed my future the night I gave myself to you. And, just because I have no future, I wish you to abide by your oath.

OLIMPIO: Your impatience might easily lead us to disaster.

BEATRICE: My impatience! But I have been patient for so many years, and this which you call impatience is but the extreme limit of long-enduring patience. What do you think? That I wish to avenge myself simply for this sojourn at La Petrella? No; I wish to avenge myself, above all, for the innocence of which my father robbed me, many, many years ago. Listen a moment! At nine years old I was an innocent child, I knew nothing of evil. In our house at that time there was a servant-maid from Spoleto called Maria Pelli, a big, tall, ugly, animal-like woman. Well, one day

when I was with this Maria Pelli in the kitchen, my
father came rushing in with a blazing, distorted face,
and without a word seized her by the hair and dragged
her into a little room next door where her pallet was
and threw her down on it. I had followed them, terrified, thinking that he intended to hurt her; and I
began beating him on the back with my fists, begging
him to leave her alone. But he paid no attention to
me, and Maria said in a faint voice: "He's not hurting
me, Beatrice, don't be frightened." And then I saw
her close her eyes and abandon herself. I stood in the
corner weeping, not from fear now, but from a kind
of shame that I did not understand. And he stayed there
on top of that woman, for as long as he wanted to,
and then he rose up and, without looking at me, said:
"Don't cry, you silly girl; one of these days you'll
be doing the same thing and you certainly won't cry
then." And so I lost my innocence, not at a fitting age,
through love, but as a child, in a manner wrong and
unseemly; and the brutal guilt of it lies at his door.

OLIMPIO: What is all this? Nothing, less than
nothing. You saw your father making love to the
servant-girl. What of that?

BEATRICE: Oh, indeed, nothing at all. For you,
nothing in life exists, except your own convenience
Even oaths—what are they? Nothing.

OLIMPIO: Ah no, that is not true.

BEATRICE: The conqueror of Lepanto trembles and is afraid! The conqueror of Lepanto, oh...! oh...!

OLIMPIO: What is this now about Lepanto?

BEATRICE: Have you not told me a thousand times how you yourself routed I don't know how many Turks at Lepanto?

OLIMPIO: It is true that I fought with honour at Lepanto.

BEATRICE: The glorious conqueror of Lepanto— all he can do is creep stealthily at night, like a robber of hen-roosts, into a girl's room, and stay there till dawn, trembling, cautious, ears strained to catch the sound of every leaf that moves—oh, the great, the glorious conqueror of Lepanto!

OLIMPIO: Now be quiet!

BEATRICE: The glorious conqueror of Lepanto!

OLIMPIO: Be quiet, or else ... (*raises his hand as if to strike her.*)

BEATRICE: Oh, you threaten me? Then I shall call my father and tell him the whole truth. Help, help!

OLIMPIO: Silence!

BEATRICE: My father shall know everything, and then you will have to act—if not to keep your oath, at least to save yourself. Help, help!

SCENE 5

BEATRICE, OLIMPIO AND FRANCESCO

FRANCESCO: Hey, what is it? Who is calling for help?

(*A long silence.*)

FRANCESCO: Who was calling for help?

BEATRICE: It was I.

FRANCESCO: Why, help? Where's the danger?

BEATRICE: Olimpio . . .

FRANCESCO: Olimpio? . . .

BEATRICE: Luckily Olimpio arrived first. A bat suddenly came down from the corner of the ceiling and flew at me. I was terrified it would fix its claws in my hair.

FRANCESCO: There are always bats here; they come in at the window. But where did it go?

OLIMPIO: It flew out again. Or it may have got hidden behind some piece of furniture.

FRANCESCO: Olimpio, what are you doing here?

OLIMPIO: Lord Francesco, I heard someone calling for help and so I came as quick as I could.

FRANCESCO: I see. But now leave me with my daughter.

OLIMPIO: As you will. (*Exit.*)

SCENE 6

FRANCESCO: Beatrice, my child, this castle, and Olimpio, and the mountains round about and my rides in the mountains, and the meals I eat and Marzio playing the guitar—the whole place, in fact, has become tedious to me.

BEATRICE: Strange indeed. Yet you said you wanted to stay up here for a year or two. And now already, after only a few months, your stay has become tedious to you.

FRANCESCO: I do not know why, but when you cried for help and I came in and saw you and Olimpio, in this room, a cold, horrible feeling of boredom gripped my heart; and all at once I knew that I could not endure this boredom any longer. I feel that I am half dead, and boredom enfolds my mind like a mist, and all that I do is drenched in boredom, and even the food that I eat here has the taste of boredom.

BEATRICE: What does boredom taste like?

FRANCESCO: It has the taste of life when nothing

comes to shake it and raise it from its normal course. A very insipid taste, to be sure.

BEATRICE: I do not know, then, what boredom is, because I do not know what life is—this normal life of which you speak.

FRANCESCO: Do not complain, I beg you. Your complaints too have become tedious to me, like Olimpio's bragging and Lucrezia's stupidity and Marzio's good sense. Your hatred for me—because you do hate me, don't deny it—stimulated me, yesterday; but today it has become tedious. What are we to do, Beatrice?

BEATRICE: I do not know what *you* ought to do. I only know what *I* ought to do.

FRANCESCO: Oh, enough, enough, enough! Always that gloomy, menacing tone, always these dark, hostile words! Enough of it! How tedious all this is! Enough!

BEATRICE: Enough, indeed.

FRANCESCO: I must change everything, invent a new life or at least a semblance of a new life; and never mind if the semblance lasts only a short time. All I want is to amuse myself for a few months— what am I saying?—a few days! I am so numbed with boredom that I would burn the house down just to warm myself for a few minutes. We must change everything; what do you say to that, Beatrice?

BEATRICE: What can be changed, now?

FRANCESCO: Everything. I began thinking about it today, during our ride. I gave a kind of shudder at the thought of it, and you noticed it and asked me whether I wasn't feeling ill. Yes, in truth I was feeling ill; it was boredom raising its head within me and fixing its poisoned tooth in my heart. And while you were saying: "You are not well; shall we go back to the Castle?" I was thinking: "Not to the Castle, but to Rome, as quick as possible." Yes, Beatrice, I made up my mind at that moment: we will go, and I'll take you back to Rome.

BEATRICE: Are you speaking seriously?

FRANCESCO: Certainly I am.

BEATRICE: We are going back to Rome?

FRANCESCO: In two or three days, at the most.

BEATRICE: Have you really decided or is this just a pretence, like last time, so as to torment me and make a mock of me?

FRANCESCO: I have decided and I shall do it. And, in order that I may hear no more complaints from you in Rome and that the tedium of this place may not occur all over again—in order, in fact, that everything may be truly changed—I shall not merely take you back to Rome but I have also decided to find you a husband as soon as possible. Your curses have become tedious to me. Let us see if your blessings are more amusing.

BEATRICE: You are taking me to Rome to find me a husband?

FRANCESCO: Yes, that is what I have decided to do.

BEATRICE: Are you quite sure you will not change your mind again?

FRANCESCO: Certain.

BEATRICE: Well, if this is true, may you be accursed once more.

FRANCESCO: No, Beatrice, no, that won't do any more. Once upon a time, as I told you, it amused me to hear myself cursed by your innocent lips, but now, alas, it bores me. You must bless me, Beatrice, if you wish to amuse me.

BEATRICE: I did not come into the world in order to amuse you.

FRANCESCO: No? What did you come into the world for, then?

BEATRICE: God alone knows that.

FRANCESCO: Beatrice, I do not want any more gloomy words from you. I want your gratitude; that will be something new for me. We'll go to Rome and find you a husband there. Beatrice, are you not grateful to me?

BEATRICE: I shall not leave this place, I shall not go to Rome, I shall not get married.

FRANCESCO: No, Beatrice, no, that is not the way you should answer me. Why, Beatrice, why should you not return to Rome, why should you not get married?

BEATRICE: Because it is too late!

FRANCESCO: It is never too late for such things.

BEATRICE: You should have told me this the day that you came up here because of that letter of mine. Now it is too late.

FRANCESCO: And what has happened in the meantime to make it too late? Nothing, nothing, nothing. You have slept, you have ridden with me in the mountains, you have eaten, you have chattered to Lucrezia. Nothing.

BEATRICE: Nothing, in very truth. Absolutely nothing.

FRANCESCO: But perhaps, Beatrice, I have not explained myself clearly.

BEATRICE: You have explained yourself extremely clearly.

FRANCESCO: No, I have not explained myself clearly; my proposal was lacking in the alluring colours of real life. Once we are in Rome, Beatrice, I wish to find you a husband according to your highest desires, a young man to your own taste, of your own position and age. And I wish your wedding to have all the splendour suitable to our rank, Beatrice. Your wedding must be one of those occasions whose magnificence is remembered for a long time. You shall be married, Beatrice, and you shall have children and be happy. Possibly your happiness will provide me with material for amusement, seeing that your unhappiness bores me so intensely.

BEATRICE: Oh, you know how to torment people not only when you wish to injure them but even when you wish to benefit them! But do you not realize that you will *not* take me away from here, that you will *not* find me a husband, and that I shall *not* have children and shall never be happy?

FRANCESCO: And why? Provided that I wish it, it shall be done.

BEATRICE: But you do not really wish these things, I mean you do not wish them with your heart. Your only wish is to relieve your boredom; and you delude yourself into thinking that you may perhaps find some amusement by indulging me. But I tell you that you will do nothing. And, even if you want to do these things, *I* shall not do them.

FRANCESCO: Why would you not do them, my little Beatrice?

BEATRICE: I have already told you: because, unfortunately, they are no longer possible. And it is you who have made them impossible.

FRANCESCO: It depends upon me, however, to make them possible again.

BEATRICE: Ah no, human beings are not puppets that can be made to act one part or another, indifferently. They are human; and if you can delude yourself into thinking that you can change everything in your own life, other people are not necessarily disposed to do the same thing—perhaps for the reason that what counts most in their lives is not simply being bored or being amused, as it does in yours.

FRANCESCO: What counts most in other people's lives?

BEATRICE: In other people's lives, I do not know; but what counted most in mine, ever since I was a small child, was to remain innocent and then later, when I grew up, to love and be loved in return and to get married and live happily with my husband and children. That is what used to count most in my life. What *used* to count; what counts most now, I had better not tell you.

FRANCESCO: Why not? Perhaps I might be able to grant your wish.

BEATRICE: Oh, no. That really is not possible.

FRANCESCO: Enough, enough, enough! I don't want to hear any more complaints and gloomy words and threatening allusions. What has been, has been. From now onwards you must love me, Beatrice. That will be a novelty for you too, and will help to shake off your boredom. You must love me first of all because I am your father, and then because I am on the point of giving complete fulfilment to all your desires.

BEATRICE: I do not love you, nor shall I ever love you; you are no longer my father and I have no desires left to which you could give fulfilment.

FRANCESCO: Beatrice, you must obey me. (*He takes her by the arm.*)

BEATRICE: Leave me alone.

FRANCESCO: You must obey me. And in this case to obey me means to love me.

BEATRICE: Leave me alone. You beat a dog and then expect it to make much of you. It will never do that again. When it sees you, it will go and hide, its tail between its legs.

FRANCESCO: A father has the right to ill-treat his daughter as much as he likes, and he still has the right to be loved by her just the same. You have got to love me.

BEATRICE: Leave me alone.

FRANCESCO: Come, tell me you love me; otherwise I shall break your arm.

BEATRICE: Leave me alone—ah! ah!—leave me alone!

FRANCESCO: Say it!

BEATRICE: Yes, yes, I love you! Leave me alone!

FRANCESCO: No, you must say: My father, I am your obedient, devoted and grateful daughter, and I love you.

BEATRICE (*kneeling*): My father, I am your obedient, devoted and grateful daughter, and I love you.

FRANCESCO: And I will go to Rome with you in a few days' time and I will be married and live happily with my husband and children.

BEATRICE: . . . And I will go to Rome with you in a few days' time and I will be married and live happily with my husband and children.

FRANCESCO: And now you must embrace me. Come —embrace me. Am I not being kind to you, have I not promised to remove you from here and find you a husband? Well then, you must show your gratitude: embrace me!

(*Beatrice obeys.*)

FRANCESCO: That's better. I believe I'm already less bored. I wonder—is it possible that doing good is amusing?

BEATRICE: Is this your "doing good"?

FRANCESCO: In any case, today at table I intend to announce these decisions of mine with the greatest solemnity to Lucrezia, Olimpio and everyone else. I will do this partly because I do not wish to change my mind. By making this announcement and calling everyone to witness, I shall to some extent prevent myself from turning back. One never knows: my character is such a fickle one. In the meantime I shall go and see whether dinner is ready. Doing good gives one the devil of an appetite. I'm hungry, I'm hungry, I'm hungry. (*Exit.*)

SCENE 7

BEATRICE AND LUCREZIA

(*Beatrice, left alone, goes over to the window and stands there looking out for some moments. Enter Lucrezia. Beatrice instantly turns round.*)

BEATRICE: You are just the person I wished to see. Olimpio must be warned: my father has discovered everything.

LUCREZIA: Lord have mercy!

BEATRICE: He told me he had seen Olimpio going into my room the other night and then coming out again later. Meanwhile he has decided that we are to leave for Rome as soon as possible.

LUCREZIA: Does he know that I know?

BEATRICE: Certainly he knows. He said: in Rome we shall settle accounts with you and with that excellent woman Lucrezia.

LUCREZIA: Ah, woe is me!

BEATRICE: However he does not mean either you or Olimpio to know that he knows. He made me swear that I would not speak either to you or to

Olimpio. He told me that, if I did so, he would kill me. He intends now to stage a little comedy of his own, pretending he is sorry for having kept us shut up here for so long. He is going to announce at table, in a few minutes' time, that he is taking us back to Rome and intends to find me a husband. But this is just a comedy and his real intentions are different.

LUCREZIA: And what are we to do? Ah, I knew things could not go on like this, I was so frightened, and now, you see—the thing that I feared has come about.

BEATRICE: He said: everyone shall have what he deserves. You two, you and Lucrezia, in Rome Olimpio and Marzio here.

LUCREZIA: Marzio too?

BEATRICE: Of course, Marzio too.

SCENE 8

BEATRICE, LUCREZIA AND MARZIO

LUCREZIA: Marzio, Lord Francesco intends to have you hanged. He has discovered all about Olimpio and Beatrice and intends to take vengeance upon everybody. He is taking us back to Rome, Beatrice and me. But you two, you and Olimpio, he means to get rid of you here.

MARZIO: Alas, alas, woe is me!

BEATRICE: He intends to stage a little comedy of his own, as though he wished to repair the wrongs he has done to us. But his real intention is to lull our suspicions and take us by surprise.

MARZIO: Ah, I did not want to know. Ah, why, why did I know?

SCENE 9

BEATRICE, LUCREZIA, MARZIO AND OLIMPIO

MARZIO: Olimpio, we must fly! Lord Francesco has discovered all about Beatrice and yourself; he has decided to take the ladies back to Rome and to kill us here, you and me, up here at La Petrella!

OLIMPIO: Gently, gently, what is all this? I have just this moment seen Lord Francesco, and he was affectionate and gave no sign of anything unusual.

LUCREZIA: That was because he does not wish you to know that he knows. He means to take you by surprise, after we have left here. He made Beatrice swear not to say anything to you. He intends to kill you. Your only course is to escape.

OLIMPIO: Beatrice, is this true?

BEATRICE: It is perfectly true. He was with me here a short time ago and he said he had seen you go into my room the other night and then come out later. And he said he was taking us away from here, to Rome. And he also said: "With you two, you and Lucrezia, we shall settle accounts in Rome. But I do not want Olimpio to suspect anything until the last moment. He has deceived me, and I shall deceive him; he has taken away my daughter's honour without my knowing it; I shall take away his life without his knowing it." In short, he intends to kill you and he intends to kill Marzio too.

OLIMPIO: I shall not go!

LUCREZIA: What will you do?

OLIMPIO: You mean, what will *we* do? He intends to kill us; we shall therefore see to it that we kill him first.

LUCREZIA: God have pity upon us!

MARZIO (*suddenly starting to wail*): Ah, poor Marzio, poor Marzio! I want to go away, I'll come back when it's all over, I do not wish to know anything, I want to go away! For the love of God, let me go, I want to go away!

OLIMPIO: Be quiet!

MARZIO: I want to go away, I want to go . . .

(*Olimpio overpowers him, throwing an arm about his neck and clapping a hand over his mouth. Almost at the same moment, the door opens and two servants come in, carrying dishes. Behind them comes Francesco.*)

SCENE 10

OLIMPIO, FRANCESCO, LUCREZIA, BEATRICE,
MARZIO AND SERVANTS

FRANCESCO (*sitting down at the table*): To table, to table! Pour out the wine, fill the glasses! Before we begin to eat, I wish to make an announcement. To table, I tell you!

(*All do as they are bid.*)

FRANCESCO: With the greatest solemnity, therefore, I make the following announcement. Item one: we leave La Petrella and go to Rome. We all leave together: I myself, Lucrezia, Beatrice, and you too, Olimpio, with your family, and you too, Marzio, with yours. Item two: you are all invited to the wedding of my daughter Beatrice which will be celebrated in Rome as soon as possible with the greatest splendour. And now I beg you to drink my health and to wish me happiness and long life.

(*All rise to their feet and drink to Francesco's health.*)

ALL: Happiness and long life!

MARZIO: It is never too late, Lord Francesco, to recognize one's own injustices and to do good.

FRANCESCO: Well said, Marzio, you have spoken the truth. It is never too late to do good.

ACT THREE

Part 1

SCENE 1

FRANCESCO, BEATRICE, OLIMPIO, MARZIO AND
LUCREZIA

(*The same room. It is evening. Francesco, Beatrice and
Olimpio are sitting at the table, which still has a few dishes,
plates, knives and forks, etc., scattered about it. Marzio
is sitting beside the fireplace. Lucrezia is clearing the table.*)

FRANCESCO: Well, have you finished your preparations?

LUCREZIA: There is little to prepare: my belongings
and Beatrice's go all into a single trunk. We have
almost nothing to prepare.

FRANCESCO: You see how you always find an excuse
for complaining? I did not ask whether you have
much stuff or little; I asked whether you were ready
to leave.

LUCREZIA: Yes, we are ready. We could leave at
once if necessary.

FRANCESCO: We shall leave tomorrow morning, at
our leisure, before midday.

LUCREZIA: It would be as well, however, if you went to bed early this evening: you have tired yourself much today in your comings and goings about the Castle. You should take a long rest. You forget you are no longer young.

FRANCESCO: What is this tale about being no longer young?

LUCREZIA: You have passed your fiftieth year.

FRANCESCO: Why, oh why did I marry such a tiresome woman? You foolish creature, you pretend to behave like a good wife but really you are not in the least concerned about me and wish merely to vex me.

LUCREZIA: Forgive me.

FRANCESCO: Yes, forgive me. But it's too late now and you have put me in an ill humour, and just when my brain was preparing itself for sleep you have opened a door into it for a number of thoughts which were only waiting for that remark of yours, "You are no longer young", to come rushing in like a swarm of filthy bats. Ah, I have been feeling all the time that something was not going right. I sat down unwillingly to table, I scarcely ate anything, and all the time an excruciating feeling of boredom has been gnawing at my heart. Oh boredom! Boredom! Boredom! It is true, I am no longer young and I'm bored into the bargain. What am I to do?

BEATRICE: You had given us to hope that you would not speak of your boredom again for some time.

FRANCESCO: The fault is yours if I am bored. I was wondering just now: why am I so bored? And then I looked at you, I saw your gloomy, discontented, hostile face and I understood. It is you, with that ill-omened face of yours, who bring back boredom into my heart.

BEATRICE: You do not know what you are saying.

FRANCESCO: Yes, you who should be cheerful, and full of gratitude and hope, inasmuch as you are about to achieve what you affirmed to be your greatest desire —to go to Rome; you who should be filled with joy seem, instead, to be filled with listlessness and discouragement.

BEATRICE: And why, pray, should I be cheerful?

FRANCESCO: Because we are leaving here and going back to Rome.

BEATRICE: If you wish, we will not go at all. I have already told you so many times: I no longer have any reason for leaving this Castle.

FRANCESCO: You have never had any reason. I myself, spurred on by boredom, have sought to change both myself and my outward life, but I must admit that your happiness—if this apathy of yours can be so called—bores me just as much as your unhappiness, if not more. Ah, Marzio, you were wrong when you said it is never too late to do good.

MARZIO: Lord Francesco, to do good is not enough: one must know how to do it.

FRANCESCO: It is clear that I do not know how to do it. But I think, on the other hand, that in certain cases it is too late to do anything, either good or evil or even the things that are neither evil nor good. Provided that such things exist.

BEATRICE: I am going to bed.

FRANCESCO: One moment, I was on the very point of speaking about you. And you want to go away?

BEATRICE: Speaking about me?

FRANCESCO: Yes, about you. Perhaps you think you can ignore what I am saying, just as a healthy man tries to ignore the complaints of a sick man? I would have you know, Beatrice, it is not only for me that it is too late to do anything, but for you too.

BEATRICE: I do not understand you.

FRANCESCO: Oh, you understand me very well indeed; we are made to understand one another, we two. Perhaps you thought I said it was too late for me because Lucrezia—inopportunely as usual— reminded me of my fifty years. If so, you were wrong. For me it was too late even at twenty, even at ten, even before I was born. And it is too late for you too, Beatrice, even though you are young and have no experience of life.

BEATRICE: I wished to go to bed and you kept me back to listen to these ravings!

FRANCESCO: I am not raving. It is too late for me and it is too late for you, Beatrice, because we are of the same family and for our family it is perhaps some centuries too late. The thing that I call boredom is, in reality, an incapacity for living, and it is an ancient heritage handed down from father to son, for hundreds of years, in the thin, tired blood of the Cenci. It meanders down from generation to generation and, like a river which at its source is a mere streamlet and then, as it flows onwards, is swollen by many tributaries, it has in no wise lessened but has increased with time, and has become, for our family, the only motive in life—if indeed the lack of all motive can be called a motive. Boredom dislocates my life, Beatrice; it makes me desire first one thing and then its opposite; but it dislocates your life even more and makes you incapable of living and of truly desiring anything. It is too late for me, Beatrice, but even more is it too late for you.

BEATRICE: You can speak for yourself. I am not like you; I do not know this boredom you speak of, and I know very well what it is I desire.

FRANCESCO: What do you mean, Beatrice? What do you mean? Would you maintain something which is so completely contrary to the truth? You are made like me, in my image and likeness, and age does not count.

BEATRICE: I tell you I am not made like you— fortunately.

FRANCESCO: Well, there is one difference between us: I know myself and I do not deceive myself. You, on the other hand, do not know yourself, and you deceive yourself about yourself.

BEATRICE: You are wrong.

FRANCESCO: I am wrong, am I? Supposing I prove it to you?

BEATRICE: You could not.

FRANCESCO: Well then, I will prove it. Let us consider. It seemed, for instance, that you wished to go to Rome at all costs. In fact you wrote that letter to your brother, declaring that, if only he would rescue you from here, you would even be prepared to take the veil. Is not that so, Beatrice?

BEATRICE: Yes, that is so.

FRANCESCO: Well, the day that you so longed for has come and all your rage has suddenly evaporated, and when I announced that we were leaving for Rome you answered me that you wished to remain here. Nor does the prospect of getting married now have the attraction that one might have supposed it had from your letter. It is I who am taking you away, I who am finding you a husband; but, if it depended on you, you would stay up here languishing in these rooms, lonely, ragged, dirty, idle, listless, for ever complaining of your situation yet never doing anything to escape from it. Is it not so, Beatrice? Is this what you call the will, the capacity, the appetite for living? At the first approach of the food you have so earnestly implored, your hunger has vanished all of a sudden and here you are recoiling in disgust even before you have tasted it. For what reason? For no reason at all, except that you are made like that. That is, you are made like me and like all the Cenci for centuries back.

BEATRICE: Your proofs prove nothing; you are wrong. I have certain excellent reasons for no longer desiring the things that I desired a few months ago.

FRANCESCO: Well then, tell me these reasons. If they are good ones, I shall be willing to admit that I have been wrong.

BEATRICE: No, I shall not tell you my reasons. This only I tell you: you speak for yourself, not for me. And if the Cenci have always been as you say—well, I am not a Cenci.

FRANCESCO: Come, Beatrice my child, do not be angry: all the more so, because getting angry when you are in the wrong is a typical Cenci characteristic. You refuse to tell me your reasons because there aren't any. And do you wish to know who is not a Cenci? Lucrezia, here—she is not a Cenci. Olimpio is not a Cenci.

LUCREZIA: Would it were true that I am not a Cenci and that I had never met you!

FRANCESCO: Lucrezia desired to go back to Rome too, but with less violence than you, Beatrice. But she still desires it—isn't that so, Lucrezia?

LUCREZIA: At least I shall be in my own house, and shall be living in a town and no longer going about in rags.

FRANCESCO: That's it: to be in one's own house, to live in a town, not to be dressed in rags. This is what Lucrezia wanted, this is what she still wants; she is not a Cenci. And Olimpio, too, is not a Cenci—isn't that so, Olimpio?

OLIMPIO: Lord Francesco, I am not one but I should like to be.

FRANCESCO: A very good answer! Yes, you would like to be one because you do not think of the boredom which runs in the very blood of our veins, but only of our riches. It is an answer which shows exactly what manner of man you are: a man of order, a reasonable man, an ambitious man who wishes to rise and to better his own condition. You wish to be better than your father, Olimpio, just as your father wished to be better than your grandfather. It is the answer of those who are not of the Cenci family. They wish for concrete things, for money, possessions, power, and they are constant in their wishes and know what it is they wish for. But you, Beatrice my child, you are like me: you do not wish for anything. And, since you do not wish for anything, it seems to you that you wish now for one thing and now for its opposite. And thus it comes about that you and I can never meet, Beatrice, for the precise reason that we are made in the same fashion: when you wish to leave here, I do not; and when I wish it, you wish to remain.

BEATRICE: I have already told you: you speak for yourself, not me.

FRANCESCO: Pride: another Cenci characteristic. You are proud, Beatrice, and you will not admit that nothing urges you to do either one thing or another. But when you reach my age you will become humbler and you will confess the truth: there is nothing, nothing, nothing.

BEATRICE: Why do you not go to bed?

FRANCESCO: I am going, Beatrice. Sleep—that is the only thing about which the Cenci, one and all, should be agreed. Sleep, sleep—sleep is the thing that most resembles death, and it is death they invoke from the moment when they enter upon life. Good-night, Lucrezia. Good-night, Beatrice. Good-night, Olimpio. Good-night, Marzio. (*Exit.*)

SCENE 2

LUCREZIA, BEATRICE, OLIMPIO AND MARZIO

LUCREZIA (*her voice trembling*): And what am I to do now?

OLIMPIO: We've explained that already: you must go to bed just as on any other night and lie down beside him. Later on Beatrice will come and call you, and then you will come out of the room and leave him alone.

LUCREZIA: Would it not be better if I stayed here all night? I know so well I shall not be able to sleep.

OLIMPIO: No, it would not be better; in that way you would arouse his suspicions and he would not sleep either, and all would have to be done over again. You must go and get into bed beside him just as on any other night.

LUCREZIA: Ah, woe is me! To lie down beside a man who is so soon to die! If I stayed here, I should feel, in a way, that I was not even an accomplice. But to lie down beside him and then get up and leave him alone, sleeping, at your mercy—that, truly, is terrible.

OLIMPIO: Come, you must go.

LUCREZIA: Beatrice, must I go?

BEATRICE: Did you not hear what Olimpio said?

LUCREZIA: Marzio, at least *you* tell me that I need not go!

MARZIO: Do you ask my opinion on such a matter? You did not ask me what I thought about the deed itself.

LUCREZIA: I will go, I will go. But it will be terrible. And it may happen that he will wish to take his pleasure with me, and that will be terrible too. But do not look at me like that, all of you! I am going, do you not see that I am going? (*Exit.*)

SCENE 3

MARZIO, OLIMPIO AND BEATRICE

MARZIO: I am going too. The Lady Lucrezia did not want to go to bed because she feared that, once she was lying beside her husband, her courage would fail her. But I, who am more afraid than she is, go willingly to my bed because the sight of my family will give me back the courage that I now lack. It is for them that I am doing it.

OLIMPIO: Be calm; I will come and call you myself.

MARZIO: Do you not see that I am perfectly calm?

OLIMPIO: Perfectly calm indeed! Your hands are trembling so much that they could almost play the guitar by themselves!

MARZIO: Who ever said that courage means not having any fear? Courage is the conquering of fear. And I will conquer it! (*Exit.*)

SCENE 4

OLIMPIO AND BEATRICE

OLIMPIO: Beatrice, you and I must speak clearly, for the last time, before it is too late.

BEATRICE: What is it you wish of me?

OLIMPIO: Beatrice, we still have the choice.

BEATRICE: You know we have no choice. My father knows about us two, and by taking me back to Rome he means to separate us and then take his revenge upon each of us.

OLIMPIO: But tomorrow morning, after you have left, I could easily mount my horse and escape. In a few hours I should be far from here, and he would never see me again.

BEATRICE: And what would become of me? Do you not think of me?

OLIMPIO: Your father could not treat you much worse than he does at present. And it may even be that he really intends to find you a husband.

BEATRICE: *You* say that to *me*?

OLIMPIO: Why, what is the matter?

BEATRICE: And so I am to go to Rome and accept as my husband the first man who is willing, in exchange for a good dowry, to accept me in return, as I now am —except that he will hold it against me for the rest of my life. *You* say that to *me*?

OLIMPIO: I do not say that you ought to do this: I say that you could do it.

BEATRICE: But it is no longer possible for me to get married.

OLIMPIO: Say rather that you do not wish to.

BEATRICE: No, I cannot, even if I wished. To have dreamed, since earliest childhood, of marriage in the way in which all girls of my age understand it, and then, instead, to have to adapt myself to a union without love, without dignity, without purity, full of lies and regrets, so that I should be compelled to blush for myself every day of my life and to envy even the poorest peasant girl who at her marriage is barefoot and homeless. Is this what I ought to accept, in your opinion? To be, in fact, a Cenci to the end of my days —if it is true, as true it is, that the Cenci never do anything that one can *not* be ashamed of, or that does not resemble a whited sepulchre, fair outside and full of corruption inside?

OLIMPIO: I do not say that.

BEATRICE: I cannot get married. I might have been what I dreamed of being, but my father prevented it and compelled me to be what I would never have wished to be. Now I wish to be what he compelled me to be, right to the end, without repentance and without regret.

OLIMPIO: Beatrice, we can all of us be so many things, according to our own wills.

BEATRICE: Oh no, no. We are the children of our actions. But why go on talking? The truth is that you are afraid and are seeking an excuse to abandon me and do nothing at all.

OLIMPIO: No, I am not afraid of what we are about to do. But I am afraid of you.

BEATRICE: Of me? Have I already reached the point of being such a fright?

OLIMPIO: Please understand me. I tell you I am not afraid of doing what we are about to do: it is necessary, for my own safety and yours, and even if this were not so, I have come to hate your father; he himself has done more to convince me than you have, with all your reasons. He is not worthy to live; possibly he is even aware of this, and in killing him we are but forwarding his destiny. But I am afraid of you because never yet have you come to a halt. The more I conceded, the more have you asked, and when

I gave you my hand you seized my arm as well. I want to be sure, Beatrice, that when we have accomplished this deed you will stop and think for once both of yourself and of me.

BEATRICE: I will stop, as you call it, only when all is finished.

OLIMPIO: These things finish only with death. I do not ask so much as that. I want only to be reassured about your intentions.

BEATRICE: It is I who need reassurance. You have many things in your life, but I have only you—if indeed that is anything.

OLIMPIO (moved): You said you have only me in your life?

BEATRICE: My life now is a very little thing, but that little is you.

OLIMPIO: Well, well, Beatrice, try to remember that, tomorrow, and you will see that all difficulties will be removed.

BEATRICE: You must go now.

OLIMPIO: Yes, I will go. In five hours' time I will come back with Marzio and as we go past your room I will knock gently, as arranged. (Exit.)

Part 2

SCENE 1

(*The same room some hours later. The flickering light of a candle appears in the doorway and then Lucrezia, in a dressing-gown, comes in holding a candlestick. She goes to the fireplace, puts down the candlestick, sits down and stays for a long time motionless, staring at the floor; then she begins to weep, groaning and lamenting in a subdued manner. Enter Beatrice, also in a dressing-gown and carrying a candlestick. She goes over to the fireplace, puts down her candlestick on the chimney-piece and looks at her stepmother.*)

BEATRICE: What are you doing here? I woke up with a start and saw you pass along the corridor like a ghost. What are you doing? Why are you weeping?

LUCREZIA: You know why I am weeping.

BEATRICE: After all perhaps it is better for us two to stay here. They won't be long now and we must not be an encumbrance to them.

LUCREZIA: Ah, I do not want to stay either here or there, but to be far away. And to know nothing.

BEATRICE: And then to hear, as if by chance, that your husband is dead, and to exclaim: "Really? Poor man! Who ever would have expected it?" Isn't that right?

LUCREZIA: Would not you, also, wish it to be so?

BEATRICE: Certainly not. I have always known everything, both what I was doing myself and what others were doing. And, of all the things I have known, this matter of his death is, perhaps, not the most terrible.

LUCREZIA: I, on the other hand, have never known anything. Things have always happened independently of my wishes, without my knowing about them.

BEATRICE: You yourself have no need to know what you are doing. All you need is for someone to tell you that what you are doing is right.

LUCREZIA: That may be true; but then you all have good reasons for doing what you are doing—Marzio because he has a half-naked, starving family and hopes to gain some advantage from it; Olimpio because he loves you; you because you have always hated *him*. But I? I was a poor widow and along came Lord Francesco and took me for his wife, and he was one of the greatest noblemen in Rome and I was nothing, and for many years he was my husband, exactly like other husbands, even if sometimes he used to beat me and go with other women. And only yesterday he and I had carnal relations, as husband and wife. And he is not displeasing to me, although I recognize that he is a terrible and a wicked man. And now he will die, and I have no reasons for wishing him to die, and I am dismayed and frightened, and I know that this thing is neither good nor right, at least for me.

BEATRICE: It is true, the thing we are about to do is neither good nor right, in fact it is a great iniquity.

LUCREZIA: Let it not be done then, for the love of God! We are still in time.

BEATRICE: It must be done. Even though it be an iniquity, it must be done.

LUCREZIA: But why, why?

BEATRICE: Because it is not possible not to do it.

LUCREZIA: I do not understand you.

BEATRICE: You would like me to tell you that the thing we are going to do is both good and right. And I could satisfy you, if I wished. I could tell you, for example, that this family of ours has lasted long enough and that when it happens in a family that the fathers are worse than the children, it is a sign that the family ought to come to an end. But I shall not tell you this.

LUCREZIA: It is not a good reason.

BEATRICE: It is a very good reason. Everything comes to an end, even families, and sometimes we are only the instruments of a nature that desires the end of all things. But as I said, I shall not tell you this. Again, I could tell you that he has deserved to die for all the wickednesses he has committed. But I shall not tell you this either.

LUCREZIA: You will not say that because you know that no one has the right to take the law into his own hands.

BEATRICE: Exactly. All I will say to you is this: it is an iniquity but it is not possible not to do it.

LUCREZIA (*suddenly rising*): I am going now into his room, and I shall give a cry and awaken him and then tell him I have had a nightmare, and so nothing will happen. I am going, yes, I am going!

BEATRICE (*seizing hold of her*): No, you are not going.

(*The two women struggle together for a moment*; *then Beatrice forces Lucrezia to her knees in front of her, so that Lucrezia's head is against her lap.*)

LUCREZIA: Let me go!

BEATRICE: No, I shall not let you go. That is the attitude in which *I* should be, kneeling with my face in the lap of a mother who loved and understood me. And in order to comfort me, this mother would perhaps gently tell me a fairy-tale. But I have told you: this is a time of trouble in which everything is upside down. And the children are better than the

145

fathers, and the stepmother kneels with her face in her stepdaughter's lap and weeps and wishes to be comforted. Would you like me to tell you a pretty fairy-tale, Lucrezia?

LUCREZIA: Ah, there are no fairy-tales for me, nor will there ever be again.

BEATRICE: Yet here is a pretty fairy-tale. Once upon a time there was a king who had a good and beautiful daughter. The queen had died when the daughter was still a child and the king had married again. The stepmother was also beautiful and good. And the king too, strange to relate, was beautiful and good. And yet, for some reason, in spite of this everything ended badly in this perfect family. The stepdaughter came to an understanding with her stepmother and with her betrothed—who also, needless to say, was beautiful and good—and all together they killed the good and beautiful king. They really did kill him, for some unaccountable reason, but it is said that they then lived happily ever afterwards.

LUCREZIA: Let me go! They've already killed him; I heard a cry over there.

BEATRICE: It cannot be so, I heard nothing.

LUCREZIA: I heard a cry, the cry of a dying man.

BEATRICE: You heard an owl. These walls are full of owls; only the other night I heard them crying.

SCENE 2

LUCREZIA, BEATRICE, OLIMPIO AND MARZIO

OLIMPIO: What is this? Why is Lucrezia on her knees like this?

BEATRICE: She is asleep.

OLIMPIO: And you—why did you come in here?

BEATRICE: Oh, do not ask so many questions! What does it matter?

OLIMPIO: In such a situation everything matters. The thing we are about to do demands great prudence.

LUCREZIA (*jumping to her feet*): You have not done it yet?

MARZIO: We have this moment arrived.

LUCREZIA: If you have not yet done it, then, for the love of God, do not do it! (*She throws herself upon Olimpio.*)

OLIMPIO: Eh, what is it now? Leave me alone.

LUCREZIA: Do not do it! This man is not evil, believe me! Only yesterday, finding himself alone with me, he said: "Lucrezia, the anniversary of our wedding is in a month's time. I intend to give you a fine present on this occasion." An evil man does not speak in that way, do you think?

OLIMPIO: Let me go, I tell you.

LUCREZIA: No, I shall not let you go until you give up your plan. He said to me, too: "I want to build a votive chapel beside the palace." A man who makes such suggestions is not evil, is he?

MARZIO: But we are not killing him because he is evil, we are killing him because the Lady Beatrice wills it.

LUCREZIA: Do not do it! Some days ago, he said to me: "I have behaved unjustly towards Olimpio who is so devoted to me and is a most courageous and honourable man. I have behaved unjustly towards him and I intend to repair the wrongs I have done him. I will confer some benefit upon him." A man who speaks like that is not evil, surely?

OLIMPIO: It is true, I am a man of honour. And what else?

LUCREZIA: He also said: "There are many noblemen in Rome who, in comparison with Olimpio, look like mere labourers."

OLIMPIO: That is true too, without any possible doubt.

LUCREZIA: Well then, if you are a nobleman, how

can you do such a thing as this? A nobleman does not kill treacherously. Do not do it, for the love of God, do not do it.

MARZIO: What are we to do?

BEATRICE: Do not do it! Go back, then, to your own homes, both of you! Slip into your warm beds again, into the arms of your wives. And make love to them too, God help you!—make love to those wives of yours who ask nothing better than to be got with child by strong men like you! All the energy you would have needed for the killing of this man—you must lodge it within the wombs of your wives and something rare will be born of it. A truly noble energy, indeed! Timorous, cowardly children will be born, who will tremble and faint at the movement of a leaf!

OLIMPIO: To whom are you speaking?

BEATRICE: To the man who is afraid, whoever he may be.

LUCREZIA: Do not do it! Pay no attention to Beatrice. She will be the first, tomorrow, to thank you for not having done it. Do not do it! Listen to the voice of conscience which is never mistaken and which bids you not to do it.

BEATRICE: Do as you wish. I shall remain your enemy for life, and you may consider that you have never seen me or known me.

OLIMPIO: I have not said anything. You can talk like that to Marzio if you wish.

MARZIO: Oh yes, talk to me, say what you wish. Tell me I am a coward, too, for in very truth I am.

OLIMPIO: But I am not, nor have I ever been. Come, Marzio.

LUCREZIA: For the love of God, do not do it!

OLIMPIO: Away, let me go! Come, Marzio! (*Exeunt Olimpio and Marzio.*)

SCENE 3

BEATRICE AND LUCREZIA

BEATRICE: The only one I am sorry for—you know who that is?

LUCREZIA: We are all worthy of pity. All of us.

BEATRICE: The only one I am sorry for is Marzio, who is doing it for love of his family. Money is not a reason, it is as nothing. And he, for nothing, will stain his hands with blood. And I am sorry for him also because, if he had been able, he would not have done it; he has been forced to it by necessity.

LUCREZIA (*going to the window and throwing it open*): It is day, already . . .

BEATRICE: At this hour that poor woman who is Marzio's wife, and her children, are still asleep in their bare hut. And he will come home later on like a wild beast that has been out in the cold all night, hunting, and that comes back at dawn to its lair, bearing its prey in its mouth. And thus Marzio's wrongdoing arises out of the love he bears his family. And that is the worst thing of all.

LUCREZIA (*looking out of the window*): Dawn is here. And there is the village with all its roofs, still asleep; not a single chimney smoking. They are all asleep, and they are all happier than I am, even the poorest, even the sick, even the dying.

BEATRICE: Others always seem to us happier than we are ourselves. Perhaps, at this moment, someone in the village sees you looking out of the window and looks up at you and thinks: "There is the Lady Lucrezia who is so much happier than I am."

LUCREZIA: Ah, woe is me, Olimpio has appeared on the balcony of the bedroom and is making a sign to me. Woe is me! Woe is me!

BEATRICE: Be quiet, it is done. Why do you cry out at the window like that? Do you wish the whole village to know of it?

LUCREZIA: Ah, woe is me, why was I not beside him and why did I not die too? What will become of me now?

BEATRICE: Ah, be quiet!

LUCREZIA: Woe is me, there they are, Olimpio and Marzio, carrying him out of the room, on to the balcony! Ah, I cannot look any longer. I would like now to pray—if I can—to pray for his soul.

BEATRICE (*going to the window and hastily shutting it*): To pray? Now is not the time to pray!

SCENE 4

OLIMPIO, MARZIO, LUCREZIA AND BEATRICE

(*Marzio is wearing Francesco's cloak, which is too ample and too long for him.*)

OLIMPIO: It is done!

LUCREZIA: Did he say anything?

OLIMPIO: As we came in, he said: "Ho there, what is it?" Then we leapt upon him and Marzio held him still and I prevented him from saying anything more.

LUCREZIA: He said nothing else?

OLIMPIO: Not a word.

LUCREZIA: Even criminals condemned to death are allowed to commit their souls into God's keeping. He did not have even that indulgence.

OLIMPIO: What ought we to have done? Should I have said to him: "Lord Francesco, you have got to die, please say your prayers"? And then waited behind the door until he had finished?

LUCREZIA: I know nothing, I have seen nothing, I have done nothing. Remember that: I know nothing.

153

OLIMPIO: So much the better: you know nothing and therefore you will say nothing.

MARZIO: Can I go home?

OLIMPIO: Yes, you can go now. What remains to be done, we will do.

MARZIO: I will come back later.

OLIMPIO: One moment, Marzio.

MARZIO: What more do you want of me?

OLIMPIO: Nothing, except that you should take off that cloak. In the first place it is well known in the village as Lord Francesco's cloak. In the second place, it is twice too wide and too long for you.

MARZIO (*taking off the cloak and putting it under his arm*): You are right; my wife will shorten it.

OLIMPIO: Marzio, anyhow I wouldn't advise you to wear it at home before it becomes known that Lord Francesco is dead. Leave it here; don't be afraid, we'll give it you in a few hours' time.

MARZIO: Once again you are right. Accursed cloak —who placed it upon my shoulders? Surely it was that same devil which tempted me to do what I have done. (*He throws the cloak on the floor and goes out.*)

BEATRICE: Did you not wish to pray, Lucrezia?

LUCREZIA: Who? I? And for whom?

BEATRICE: For anyone you wish: for him, or for us, or just for yourself. Provided you go away and I do not see that frightened face of yours, at least for a few hours.

LUCREZIA: Ah, so now that all is over, you wish to have nothing more to do with me.

BEATRICE: Did you not say that you knew nothing?

LUCREZIA: I am afraid, now, to be left alone. I know nothing, it is true, I do not wish to know anything; but I beg you to act as though I did know, and do not leave me alone.

BEATRICE: What are you afraid of? Go, go away and pray, if you can. And pray for *me*, then; thus you will no longer feel that you are alone, and by praying for me you will feel close to me, if that can be any comfort to you. But go, for the love of God, go!

LUCREZIA: Why are you so angry? I am going; and I will pray for you, yes, I will pray for you as you tell me. (*Exit.*)

SCENE 5

OLIMPIO AND BEATRICE

OLIMPIO: Beatrice, what is it? You are trembling all over.

BEATRICE: I am trembling with rage. Lucrezia, with her whimperings, is capable of driving me mad.

OLIMPIO: Beatrice, from this moment you must allow yourself to be guided completely by me. If you do all that I tell you to do, in a short time we shall succeed in turning this disorder into order, this loss into gain, and what may still, at present, appear an evil action into a good one. All I desired was what you desired. But now that everything has come to pass, I will not draw back; rather, I wish to take all upon my own shoulders—on condition, however, that you help me with your obedience and your approbation.

BEATRICE: Tell me what I must do.

OLIMPIO: In the first place, we must see that our hearts are not dissevered from our actions, so that while, for instance, we show ourselves to others with calm, serene movements, our hearts are all the time trembling and afraid within us. What we have done, we have done by an action that evaded nothing, an action in which we were involved heart and soul. So it must be also in the future. That is the first thing I ask of you, Beatrice. Only if we can remain inwardly calm and serene can we appear so outwardly.

BEATRICE: I will strive to be calm.

OLIMPIO: That is well. Now I will go to bed, and you must do the same and try to rest. Then, as we agreed, as soon as it is full daylight you and Lucrezia are to discover the disaster; you are to come to the windows and cry out in such a way that the whole village hears you. I have made a large enough hole in the floor of the balcony for it to be easily supposed that he could have fallen through it. Remember, then, it was an accident: he rose from his bed and went out on to the balcony, to take the air, perhaps. The wooden flooring of the balcony, being rotten, gave way beneath his feet and he plunged through into the vegetable-garden below and was killed on the spot. You can also confirm that Lucrezia heard him exclaim "Jesus! Jesus!" just as he fell.

BEATRICE: Am I to say that?

OLIMPIO: Yes, you must say that—neither more nor less. Our behaviour must be like a well-constructed machine, in which nothing is left to chance. If you were constructing a machine, would you put into it some useless piece of apparatus, some little wheel that would not turn? Of course not. Well, you must not allow yourself to be alarmed by the fact that this is a question of human beings and not of mechanical apparatus. They will appear to you as human beings, unless you are able to fit them together in your mind and bring them into play the one with the other— just like the parts of a machine, in fact. But if you keep this idea of a machine clearly in mind, untrammelled by assaults of feeling, you will very soon perceive that human beings can indeed be parts of a machine and can be brought into play one with another for your own advantage, and according to your own needs and your own designs.

BEATRICE: Yes, I see—a machine.

OLIMPIO: We must trust in our minds because we are men and not beasts. It is true that, like beasts, we have feeling, and as long as we are doing things that beasts also do we can, if we please, abandon ourselves to feeling. But, in so far as we wish to conduct ourselves as human beings, we must leave feeling aside and rely solely on our minds.

BEATRICE: Yes, we must rely on our minds.

OLIMPIO: Hitherto we have acted in accordance with a clear-cut plan and so we must continue to act in future. Man, unfortunately, is subject to the blows of fortune and to the fits and starts of his own humour:

otherwise it would perhaps be possible to make exact plans, I do not say for the whole of life, but at any rate for a long period of years.

BEATRICE: Yes, a long period of years.

OLIMPIO: What is the matter, Beatrice? You are pale and you are still trembling. And you do not seem to hear me; you repeat mechanically the last few words I say, as though you did not understand. What is the matter?

BEATRICE: In very truth, I do not understand you.

OLIMPIO: Perhaps I did not speak clearly?

BEATRICE: Oh yes, you spoke clearly.

OLIMPIO: Why do you not understand me, then?

BEATRICE: Forgive me. But all the time you were speaking, I found it impossible to listen to you. I heard the sound of your voice but I could not catch the meaning of your words. My mind was elsewhere, and I neither heard nor understood anything.

OLIMPIO: What were you thinking of?

BEATRICE: I was looking at you, and I saw reflected in you, as if in a looking-glass, an image of myself which I should prefer not to recognize. And I said to myself that you too, as you spoke to me, saw reflected in me, as in another, similar looking-glass, an image of yourself which perhaps you already hate. And I felt that you were making a supreme effort not to see this image of yourself, and to deceive yourself into thinking that everything had remained as it was. And it seemed to me that you were all the time conscious that this effort was in vain and that there could now no longer be anything between us. And I felt lonely.

OLIMPIO: But I was not making any effort. All that I said to you I have always thought, and I shall always think it.

BEATRICE: It seemed to me, on the contrary, that you were trying to deceive me and to delude yourself that you loved me, whereas in reality I already fill you with horror, just as you were filled with horror by the image of yourself that you saw reflected in me.

OLIMPIO: I saw nothing but the Beatrice whom I have loved and whom I still love.

BEATRICE: There are some tests which even the strongest love cannot withstand; like a green log on the fire, it splits asunder. And the lovers separate and each burns on his own. Are you sure you do not desire, in your heart of hearts, never to see me again, to break free from me?

OLIMPIO: I have nothing more to say than what I have said already.

BEATRICE: I feel alone with myself. And what I am seems to be reduced to what I have done. And so I feel alone with what I have done.

OLIMPIO: We will do other things.

BEATRICE: Is it true that I do not fill you with horror? Is it really true? For if I filled you with horror, I should be filled with horror myself. And then I I should throw myself headlong to death, to death where there is nothing, neither horror nor anything else.

OLIMPIO: Be calm; I shall not leave you, we will live together.

BEATRICE: We will live together? Together, yes, we shall be together; but shall we live? Shall we be able to live after all we have done?

OLIMPIO: Do you know what this is?

BEATRICE: What do you mean?

OLIMPIO: This is your old instinct for introducing doubt and dismay into the minds of others. But this time I shall not listen to you. Think as you wish but do not tell it me: I want to know nothing more.

BEATRICE: Is it you that answers me like this?

OLIMPIO: There is the sun! Go now to your room. I shall go to my house and then, as soon as I hear you cry out, as we have agreed, I shall come back to the Castle. (*Exit.*)

Epilogue

SCENE 1

OLIMPIO AND MARZIO

(*The hall of the Castle, windows open, brilliant sunshine. Olimpio is in travelling dress and Marzio is wearing Francesco's cloak.*)

OLIMPIO: Everything is going in the best possible way, Marzio, as indeed I foresaw and intended and arranged. It is already some days since Lord Francesco was enclosed in his tomb in the church of Santa Maria della Petrella—peace be to his soul, if it is possible for such a soul to find peace anywhere. The enquiry has confirmed, in every respect, our declarations concerning the accident of which he was the victim. And today we leave for Rome, as had been decided. Even the weather favours us: it is a glorious day. Why then, O bird of ill omen, why that gloomy, frightened face?

MARZIO: Olimpio, I live in the village and not at the Castle. And in the village there is a great murmuring and people are saying plainly and openly that Lord Francesco was not the victim of an accident but was murdered.

OLIMPIO: What then?

MARZIO: What do you mean, "what then"? Isn't that enough?

OLIMPIO: If I were you, I should not trouble myself unduly about these murmurings. It is right that it should be so. Everyone knew of the ill-treatment inflicted by the father upon his daughter, and it is natural that they should now say that his daughter arranged to have him murdered. But, Marzio, these murmurings are like the circles made by a stone that falls into the water of a pond: violent at first, they become feebler and feebler, and then in the end the water becomes smooth again and the stone lies still at the bottom.

MARZIO: You think they will die down?

OLIMPIO: They are bound to die down. It is in the nature of things to lose force with the passage of time. I had taken these murmurings into account, like all the rest. I had never deceived myself that people would not murmur. But just as an architect, when he is making a house, calculates how much weight must be supported by each stone in the floor and calculates it generously so as to have no surprises when the building is finished, so did I work out my story of the accident to be even sturdier and more credible than it need be, so that it could, in fact, stand up to anyone who contested it. And so it has been. People have murmured, they have even gone and poured out their tale to the judge; but the story has held, and the judge has declared the murmurers to be wrong and us to be right.

MARZIO: That may be. But I would not like these murmurings, going from mouth to mouth, to reach as far as Rome. Roman justice is a different thing from justice up here. It is an easy matter to re-open a criminal enquiry, Olimpio.

OLIMPIO: They will not re-open it. Once in Rome, we will contrive to prevent this chatter from passing the bounds of mere gossip, and in the end it will die down like a fire without fuel. The Cenci family is powerful and has ties of blood with the greatest families in Rome. We will represent this chatter as an affront and a calumny against the Cenci and the families to whom they are related. Through the Cenci and their relations we shall exercise authority at many points and, if necessary, we shall secure the intervention of some person of influence and weight. But I am convinced, Marzio, that we shall not have to go to such lengths. Some years ago I killed an innkeeper in a quarrel. What did I do? I remained in hiding for some time, at the same time placing myself under the exalted protection of the Lord Colonna. When the uproar died down, I reappeared, and here I am, safe and sound.

MARZIO: Lord Francesco was not an innkeeper.

OLIMPIO: But everyone had seen me kill the innkeeper. No one, on the other hand, can say he saw me kill Lord Francesco.

MARZIO: You seem very sure of yourself.

OLIMPIO: In the first place, experience makes me sure: any soldier will tell you what I also tell you: that to kill a man is not after all such a terrible thing. And then, in the second place, reason: in all this affair I have so far done nothing that was not rational.

MARZIO: All the same, you only partly reassure me. You say you foresaw everything and took everything into calculation. But your foresight and calculation cannot have extended to the things that lie in the heart of man.

OLIMPIO: And what things can lie in the heart of man?

MARZIO: Fear, remorse, discouragement, horror—all of them things that you cannot foresee and that may at any moment bring to nought all your carefully arranged plans.

OLIMPIO: I promised you, I thought of this too. And in the end I said to myself that such feelings must and can be taken into calculation as far as possible. The chief resource upon which I have relied is the instinct of self-preservation which is so very strong in all men. Certainly it is possible for a man to have these feelings in his heart, but no one, I believe, would be so mad as to risk his life in order to give vent to them and so be rid of them.

MARZIO: Are you quite sure of that?

OLIMPIO: As far as it is possible to be sure of such things. And I confess to you, Marzio, that my greatest preoccupation has been Beatrice, even though it was she who willed that what has been done should be done. I was not ignorant of how inconstant she is, how rash, how passionate, how violent.

MARZIO: I warned you—do you remember? I said to you: "Be careful, you imagine that you control her whereas it is she who leads you where she wishes."

OLIMPIO: And you in your turn must remember how I answered you—that I felt myself capable of stopping her. And now, Marzio, facts have proved me right.

MARZIO: Truly?

OLIMPIO: Yes, truly. At first it seemed as though her reason were wavering like a candle-flame in a strong puff of wind. Her talk was disconnected, and even though she conformed to my instructions it was clear that her mind was filled with confusion and discouragement and passion. She was able to answer the judge; but she was not able to escape from that other judge who, according to her, was established in

166

her conscience. Continually she would declare that we had committed a great crime, and that, whatever the reasons for which we had committed it, the crime itself remained inexpiable. Then again, such was her confusion of mind that she appeared to have lost sight of the end we had in view: she kept repeating, incessantly, that her life was finished and that her father, in his fall, had dragged her down with him.

MARZIO: Perhaps she was telling the truth.

OLIMPIO: No, she was simply being sincere; and truth that is the child of sincerity or of passion may equally well be completely true or completely false. Anyhow, I was dismayed because I know that there is in her a very dangerous capacity for violence: that same violence which had made her so inflexible in desiring the death of her father, might now make her equally inflexible in desiring her own destruction and ours.

MARZIO: Now you begin to frighten me.

OLIMPIO: If I wish to frighten you, it is only to reassure you the better, afterwards. What would you have done in my place?

MARZIO: I do not know; I should have tried to reason, to convince her.

OLIMPIO: And you would have added fuel to the flames. No; I proceeded in quite a different way.

Whenever she showed signs of alluding to her father's death, I changed the subject. If she persisted, I told her to be silent. In short, I absolutely forbade her to make any allusion, even the slightest, to what has happened. In the meantime I endeavoured to make her resume her old habits, to do the things she had always done and in exactly the same way: eating, walking, looking after the house, making plans for the future, sleeping. The normal course of life, Marzio— that was the oil I poured, again and again, upon those troubled waters.

Marzio: And did you succeed in calming them?

Olimpio: I have not finished. I know that the body feeds these violent humours with the same energy with which it nourishes the passion of love. And I have noticed that when a man is satiated with love, he has little strength left for devoting himself to anything else. I set out, therefore, to exhaust Beatrice. I love her, Marzio, and this love, instead of diminishing after what has happened, has increased, in such a way that I could no longer do without her. So it was easy for me to make love to her as before and more than before; and I must tell you, Marzio, that the mingling of sadness with desire is strange but also alluring. During these last nights Beatrice, with all her violence and despair, has always ended by yielding to me and returning my rapturous caresses with ardour. One moment she would be cursing her life; and a moment later she would be responding with tireless alacrity to my embraces. Sadness of spirit, in her, has been unable to resist the joy of the body; and, the greater the admixture of sadness, the more unbridled her joy has seemed to become. The night would begin with tears, protests, distaste, frenzies of rage, to end in full and violent surrender. Everything in her rebelled against love and at the same time everything in her encouraged it, and thus there was desire in her rage, wantonness in her remorse, sensuality in her dejection; just as there was melancholy in her eagerness, grief in her caresses and fear in her surrender. In the morning she would be wearier than the night, paler than the dawn, colder than the air of these mountains. And then finally, exhausted, she would relinquish her sense of guilt and find innocence again in sleep.

MARZIO: And what has been the result of all this cleverness of yours?

OLIMPIO: There has been an excellent result, Marzio. Drained every night of the force that would have been needed, by day, to nourish her violence and impose it upon my will, she has gradually become calmed and weakened and soothed. She has made no further allusion to her father's death, not because she did not wish to do so, but rather from impotence. Those phantoms which during the first days seemed to her so alive and so menacing have gradually receded from her mind and have become pale and bloodless; in the end they have allowed mild and reassuring reality to show its face through the mists they created. She has said nothing further; but hers has been a silence of exhaustion, not of menace. Even if she wished it, she would not now have the strength to grow desperate; and if, before, every smile required an effort of falsity, today she would have to make the same effort in order to rediscover a true note of sadness. In short, Marzio, all our troubles come from not wishing to accept things as they are and hankering after things as they ought to be. Accepting means restoring to the reality that surrounds us the life which our dreams have extracted from it. It means passing from one world to another, from the world of impotence and frenzy to that of achievement and satisfaction. So much have I accomplished that I have succeeded in driving Beatrice—like a restive beast that will not re-enter the sheepfold—out of her first world of rage and violence into the second. By now she has accepted it; the rest will come of itself.

MARZIO: You are telling me, then, that we have nothing to fear from the direction of Lady Beatrice?

OLIMPIO: Nothing whatever. The wild horse has found its rider. A few days more and it will bear the saddle willingly.

MARZIO: Yes, but perhaps only for some time. Remorse is like those rivers which plunge down into a cleft in the ground, and you think the earth has swallowed them up, and then they come bursting forth again with redoubled force, a great distance away. I would not wish Beatrice to remember having killed her father when the rest of us have already forgotten it.

OLIMPIO: I am counting upon the permanent extinction of all remorse by the grafting of a new, smiling, secure life upon the shattered stump of the old. I shall not limit myself to making love to her at night, Marzio; I shall seek to give her, by day too, some reason for rewarding my nocturnal love with gratitude. We will go to Rome now and stay quietly there until the clamour caused by this death comes to an end. Then I shall send back my wife to her own village of Anticoli, to her parents' house, and I shall arrange for her to remain there together with my children. I myself, with Beatrice, expect to stay on only a short time in Rome; having settled my family, I shall go with her to Venice, or perhaps Milan. I have friends everywhere and so has Beatrice, and it will not be difficult to find protection and hospitality and to live as husband and wife without anxieties of any kind for the future. The days will pass, Marzio, and the seasons and the years; and life, like a snake that is always young and always green, will change its skin many and many a time, and Beatrice will no longer be the woman she is today or the woman she was yesterday but someone else. And I want to have children by her, so that, after the sweetness of love she shall know the sweetness of motherhood and this new sweetness shall wipe away even the memory of past bitternesses. The girl will then, at last, become a woman, and will give her breast to the child that has been conceived in her own womb; and all this, as you know, changes not only the body but the mind, and adapts it more and more closely to life. In short, Marzio, there will be nothing of importance in our future except the things that nature ordains. But Beatrice, luckily, is still so young that nature may yet ordain many things for her.

SCENE 2

OLIMPIO, MARZIO AND LUCREZIA

LUCREZIA: We cannot leave now! We are all lost!

OLIMPIO: What do you mean?

LUCREZIA: Ah, I knew they would not believe the story of the accident. I always said so. You know who is on his way here?

OLIMPIO: Who?

LUCREZIA: Don Carlo Tirone. And you know who Don Carlo Tirone is? The man who brought me the news explained to me. Don Carlo Tirone is Chief Justice of the Province of the Abruzzi, and he is a terrible man who believes nothing and nobody, who spares nobody and puts everyone to the torture and extorts confessions from everybody. I tell you, we are lost!

OLIMPIO: Gently now! How did you come to know this?

LUCREZIA: I was told it by a pedlar who saw him yesterday evening at the inn called La Pace, fifty miles from here, where he was spending the night. This pedlar spoke to one of his retinue and found out that Don Carlo Tirone was coming up here on purpose to re-open the inquest. He is on the way now and it will not be long before he arrives. Ah, I knew we should never be able to leave this accursed place.

MARZIO: Well, Olimpio, here is an event which you had neither foreseen nor taken into account.

OLIMPIO: Did this pedlar bring the news at the direct order of Don Carlo Tirone, or by chance, without any instructions?

LUCREZIA: He told me casually, without any instructions, but in a malicious, knowing sort of manner. He peered into my face all the time to see what effect it was having.

OLIMPIO: By chance then, and without instructions. Therefore we leave, as decided.

LUCREZIA: We leave?

OLIMPIO: Certainly we leave. We are not necessarily to know that Don Carlo Tirone is coming here. We have decided to leave, and leave we shall.

LUCREZIA: And what is the use of our leaving?

OLIMPIO: So that we shall not encounter Don Carlo Tirone; and so that we shall gain time. Don Carlo Tirone is a Justice of the Kingdom of Naples. We shall cross into the Papal States today. He will carry out his enquiry as best he can and then go back to Naples. In the meantime we shall be in Rome.

LUCREZIA: I do not wish to know anything; you tell me that we shall leave and that is enough. To leave —yes, to leave here is all I wish.

OLIMPIO: But we must waste no time. Are the horses already waiting in the courtyard? Go and give orders for the baggage to be brought down immediately. Marzio, you go with Lucrezia and help her. I will see about warning Beatrice.

MARZIO: Come, come, let us go.

OLIMPIO: One moment, Marzio, Lucrezia! If by chance you meet Beatrice, do not say anything to her of the arrival of Don Carlo Tirone. Not a word!

MARZIO: Set your mind at rest. (*Exeunt Lucrezia and Marzio.*)

SCENE 3

OLIMPIO AND BEATRICE. *Later*, MARZIO AND LUCREZIA

BEATRICE: And so this day has come at last.

OLIMPIO: What day?

BEATRICE: The day of departure for Rome.

OLIMPIO: Yes, it has come. Are you ready? Salute this hall for the last time, for you will never see it again. Let us go now. (*Starts to move away.*)

BEATRICE: One moment!

OLIMPIO: What is it? Are you not ready?

BEATRICE: I am ready, yes.

OLIMPIO: Well then, let us go. It is late, and we have a long journey. Come!

BEATRICE: I said I was ready. But not to do what you think.

OLIMPIO: What is it, Beatrice? What is the matter? But now let us be going. We will talk about everything on the way; we shall have time for that.

BEATRICE: No, let us talk of it now.

176

OLIMPIO: Now? But we have only a few minutes. What can be said in a few minutes, Beatrice, what can be said?

BEATRICE: Oh, plenty of things can be said. We have stayed up here for more than two years, and now are you unwilling to wait for a few minutes longer?

OLIMPIO: Speak then, seeing that you wish to do so. But have we not said everything to each other already? What is the matter? Are you frightened of going to Rome?

BEATRICE: No.

OLIMPIO: Are you frightened of the murmurings there have been up here with regard to your father's death? Do not fear, everything will come right.

BEATRICE: I am not frightened of anything.

OLIMPIO: What is it, then? Speak! Why don't you speak? What is the matter with you?

BEATRICE: You tell me to speak and at the same time you are in such a hurry that you prevent me. There is nothing wrong with me and nothing is the matter. I only wished to say this to you . . .

OLIMPIO: What?

BEATRICE: That if you wish it, we can leave here together. But, before we reach Rome, we must separate.

OLIMPIO: If that is all you wish, well and good. It would be more prudent. But now let us go.

BEATRICE: Wait, you did not let me finish: we must separate and never see each other again.

OLIMPIO: Never again? But what does this mean?

BEATRICE: It means that our love is finished.

OLIMPIO: Our love is finished?

BEATRICE: Or rather, I should say, our conspiracy is finished—of which love was but one of the aspects, perhaps not even the most important. Our love was never anything but the flattering mask that iniquity made use of to effect an entry within these walls. Having achieved its purpose, it has dropped the mask and shown its true countenance. To be brief, look to your own safety and do not concern yourself any more with me.

OLIMPIO: These are obscure words. What do you mean, Beatrice? We love each other; only last night we made love; and now our love is finished, and I am to look to my own safety. Is something threatening me, then?

BEATRICE: Do you remember, that morning, I asked you: do I not fill you with horror?

OLIMPIO: Yes; and I answered that you were dreaming.

178

BEATRICE: But alas, there was one thing I had not foreseen.

OLIMPIO: What was that?

BEATRICE: That, in the end, *you* would fill *me* with horror.

OLIMPIO: I—I?

BEATRICE: Yes, you. And, even more than you, that part of me which you have succeeded in conquering and making like yourself. You wish me to live according to your own idea of what is normal; and you do not realize that there is nothing so horrifying as a mixture of normality and crime. To go for a walk, and to think: I am walking with the man who helped me to kill my father. To eat, and to think: I am sitting at table with the man who helped me to kill my father. To lie in bed together, and to think: I am taking my pleasure with the man who helped me to kill my father. Crime is more endurable in the midst of despair and terror than in the dull placidity of everyday habits. What does all this mean? On the morning of the crime I felt myself innocent, but since then I have felt more and more guilty as the days passed and as we returned to what you call the normal course of life. Now I do not want to feel guilty, since I am not guilty. And your normality that accepts the crime and feeds upon it fills me with horror, as an everlasting hypocrisy which I could neither dismiss nor forget.

OLIMPIO: We are what we do, Beatrice. Perhaps there will not be any hypocrisy except at the first beginning of this new life of ours. Then you will come inwardly to resemble your outward actions. You will have no need to make a pretence of normality: you will be normal.

BEATRICE: It is precisely that which fills me with horror; it is that which I do not want. You know what it was that I wished to avenge upon my father?

OLIMPIO: I only know that to discuss such things, at this moment, is madness. Let us be going. We shall have plenty of time for explanations in Rome.

BEATRICE: No, we must have our explanations here, and for the last time. It was my innocence I wished to avenge. And now you want me to lose this innocence a second time, and for ever, by becoming your concubine, by following you about Italy and giving you children and living with you as husband and wife, in a normal way. This I will not do. I wish to preserve at least the hope of finding my innocence again, some day.

OLIMPIO: But how can you, Beatrice? You will never again be what you once were. And you cannot nullify the thing you have done except by doing other, completely different things.

BEATRICE: It is as you say. By doing other things. But not the things *you* want me to do.

OLIMPIO: What things then, my love?

BEATRICE: Innocence is perhaps to be found at the far end of a road that leads me irreparably away from you. The normal life of which you speak stinks of crime and complicity and hypocrisy. In that letter I wrote I said that I wished to be married or else I would go into a convent. I shall never be able to be married now. But once I am back in Rome I shall be able to find a convent that will welcome me.

OLIMPIO: You—*you*—really wish that?

BEATRICE: Yes.

OLIMPIO: Normal life with me would be hypocrisy —eh? But a veil covering that body which only last night was pressed against mine, and that head which until the other day was full of murderous thoughts— this is different, this would not be hypocrisy. Come, let us go; why should we linger over these absurdities?

BEATRICE: I do not know what it would be. I only know that I should withdraw myself from the world and find a rule of discipline, that each hour of the day I should mortify myself in obedience, humble myself in prayer, nullify myself in sacrifice, as all nuns do, both those who have done nothing wrong and those who have already lived a life full of faults. By living with them, and living as they live, without hypocrisy because I should be living in the presence of God and with God there can be no hypocrisy, I am confident that some day I shall again find the good thing which you would wish me to renounce—by which I mean innocence. Even if I did not find it, I should be satisfied with the hope of finding it; and this indeed I shall hope for, fervently, with all my soul. With you, on the other hand, there would be no possibility of cherishing such a hope.

OLIMPIO: My world is crumbling all about me. Ah, I know that if this did not take me thus unawares, and if there were not this hurry of departure, I should find a way to drive these foolish notions from your mind and to convince you once again. But I am caught unprepared, with the horses already saddled in the courtyard.

BEATRICE: No, do not deceive yourself; you would not have convinced me even if I had warned you beforehand and we had had the leisure to speak of it calmly. I am still what I was when I came up to this place, Olimpio, and I do not wish to change myself in order to please you. I am still the girl who, on the day of the crime, looked in dismay at her bloodstained hands and wondered why it should be that reason led to wrongdoing, purity to corruption, desire for happiness to unhappiness. We two have nothing in common, Olimpio, except our guilt. Therefore we must part. But if I were you I should not go to Rome; I should take the road into the mountains.

OLIMPIO: What do you mean? You intend to denounce me?

BEATRICE: I shall never do anything that might injure you. But if you do not trust me, kill me. I cannot bring death to myself, but I would willingly accept it. Do it at once: I shall be grateful to you.

OLIMPIO: No, even for that it is too late. I think I foresaw everything except that you would not wish to go on living. For that is what your new decision means, Beatrice: not to go on living.

BEATRICE: Go, Olimpio! I advise you to escape through the mountains, not because I intend to betray you, but because one can never know what may happen in a case like this. I shall go back to Rome and do what I have said. And if I cannot do it, so much the worse for me. But at least you will not be there and I shall not injure you.

OLIMPIO: A nun. And I shall never see you again.

BEATRICE: Do the dead perhaps meet again? For you, I shall be dead.

OLIMPIO: It is late, it is late, late. Farewell.

(*Olimpio goes out. Voices are heard beneath the open window. Someone shouts all of a sudden*: "Olimpio, Olimpio!" *Then there is the sound of a horse's hooves receding into the distance. Shortly afterwards Marzio and Lucrezia come in, panting for breath.*)

LUCREZIA: Olimpio has fled! He jumped on his horse and galloped off.

BEATRICE: He has gone away, he has not fled. And in a short time we shall be going too.

MARZIO: No. We shall not be going.

BEATRICE: What do you mean, Marzio? The horses are all ready.

MARZIO: We shall not be going. Don Carlo Tirone is here.

SCENE 4

BEATRICE, LUCREZIA, MARZIO, TIRONE AND
OTHERS

*(Enter Carlo Tirone, followed by his retinue and many of
the villagers. The hall fills with people.)*

TIRONE: Who was that man who, just as we reached
the open space in front of the Castle, mounted his
horse and galloped off without heeding our summons?

BEATRICE: You ought to know, since it seems you
already know everything. It was my lover, Olimpio
Calvetti, Governor of the Castle.

TIRONE: He will not go far: I have already given
instructions for two of our men to be sent after him
to stop him. In the meantime, no one is to leave this
room, no one is to move, no one is to speak to anyone
else.

LUCREZIA: But we are just leaving for Rome.
What is all this? The horses are already saddled.

TIRONE: You will remain here as long as justice
requires.

185

BEATRICE: So you come in the name of justice? What justice?

TIRONE: The justice of the Kingdom of Naples. Beatrice Cenci, you are accused of having killed, or caused to be killed, your father Francesco. Lucrezia Cenci, you are accused of having participated in the crime. Marzio Catalano, you are likewise accused of the killing of Francesco Cenci.

BEATRICE: Accuse me, if you wish. But I am innocent.

TIRONE: Parricide! When your hands are still stained with blood, do you dare proclaim your innocence?

BEATRICE: According to *your* justice you will certainly be able to prove I am guilty of my father's death. But you will never be able to prove that I am not at the same time innocent according to another justice—a justice which you can neither know nor, even less, administer. Nevertheless you come at the right moment, Signor Tirone. Everything here has been calling for your arrival, demanding your presence. Now that you are here, some kind of order will no doubt be restored. And so, what are you waiting for? Why do you not take me away?

TIRONE: I am waiting for justice to take its course.

BEATRICE: Yes, you are right, justice must take its course, whichever justice it may be. Let us go.

TIRONE: Follow her, see that she does not try to kill herself. She may seek to do so and thus fulfil the destiny of her family, which by this crime has determined its own end. This hall has seen things that would make the royal court of Mycenae turn pale. Nothing remains now but to leave it, a place henceforward sacred to divine justice, mysterious, inscrutable, which has decreed the downfall and destruction of the Cenci.